LIVING LIFE
OUT LOUD

22 INSPIRING

LIVING LIFE

NEW ZEALAND WOMEN SHARE

OUT LOUD

THEIR WISDOM

KAY DOUGLAS

Foreword by the Right Honourable Helen Clark

HarperCollins*Publishers (New Zealand) Limited*

The author and publishers wish to thank and acknowledge the following individuals and organisations who have provided photographs:

Dee McMahom, *Her Business* magazine, for Melissa Clark-Reynolds (page 17) and Soala Wilson (page 206); John Selkirk, for Sonja Davies (page 33), Leilani Joyce (page 55), Judi Grace (page 99), Barbara Kendall (page 139) and June Mariu (page 190); Theresa Gattung (page 41), photographer John Daley; Sally Synnott, (page 63); Vicki Buck (page 79); Caron Taurima (page 87); Barbara Koziarski (page 107); Jill Mitchell (page 117); Kapka Kassabova (page 127), photographer Bruce Foster; Sue Bradford (page 147); Ces Lashlie (page 158), photographer Heather Busch; Merepeka Raukawa-Tait (page 171); Sukhi Turner (page 181), photographer Elizabeth Goodall; Sue Kedgley (page 196); Lois Muir (page 218), photographer Gil Hanly; Hinewehi Mohi (page 229), photographer Jae Frew and David White, *New Zealand Herald*, for his photograph of Lucy Lawless (page 238).

The author and publishers have made every effort to trace copyright holders. If any have been inadvertently overlooked, they will be pleased to make the necessary arrangements at the first opportunity.

First published 2001
Reprinted 2001
HarperCollins*Publishers (New Zealand) Limited*
P.O. Box 1, Auckland

ISBN 1 86950 378 3
Set in Perpetua
Designed and typeset by Chris O'Brien/Pages LP
Printed by Griffin Press, South Australia, on 80 gsm Ensobelle

CONTENTS

DEDICATION

This book is dedicated to the twenty-two very special women
who shared their stories with such generosity, grace and aroha:
Sue Bradford, Vicki Buck, Melissa Clark-Reynolds,
Sonja Davies, Theresa Gattung, Judi Grace,
Leilani Joyce, Kapka Kassabova, Sue Kedgley,
Barbara Kendall, Barbara Koziarski, Ces Lashlie,
Lucy Lawless, June Mariu, Jill Mitchell,
Hinewehi Mohi, Lois Muir, Merepeka Raukawa-Tait,
Sally Synnott, Caron Taurima, Sukhi Turner
and Soala Wilson.

And to women seeking direction,
those with a cherished dream they would love to fulfil,
those who are already following their passion
and most especially to women,
who because of life's adversities,
barely dare to dream.

ACKNOWLEDGEMENTS

My deepest gratitude to the women who shared their passion, life experiences and insights for this book in the hope that their stories would encourage other women to boldly pursue their dreams. Without their generosity *Living Life Out Loud* would not have been created. Each holds a special place in my heart.

My sincere appreciation also to the Rt Hon Helen Clark who found the time in her busy schedule to write the Foreword.

Although this book has been a joy to create, it has not been without its challenges. My loving thanks to my husband John Bailey for the countless ways he has supported me in this project, including taking over extra household tasks to allow me time to write, and word processing for me when my OOS (Occupational Overuse Syndrome) was beginning to flare up.

Thank you also to my children Robert, Jenny and Angela Clancy for their encouragement, support and enthusiasm about this book and to Hannah and Thomas Bailey, my stepchildren, for tolerating my long writing periods behind closed doors.

Special thanks to Karen Coulton whose many hours of skilful transcription of the taped interviews made this book possible. I would also like to acknowledge the staff at Takapuna Library for assisting me with my research with such patience and courtesy, even though I usually visited during their peak times.

My appreciation to *Her Business* magazine for allowing me to use their photos of Melissa Clark-Reynolds and Soala Wilson; to John Selkirk for his photos of Sonja Davies, Leilani Joyce, Judi Grace, Barbara Kendall and June Mariu; to Gil Hanly for her photo of Lois Muir and to Cathy White of Greenstone Pictures for providing the photo of Hinewehi Mohi.

I am grateful to the HarperCollins team for sharing my vision and excitement about *Living Life Out Loud* and their cheerful and skilled assistance in bringing it so beautifully into being.

FOREWORD

BY THE RT HON HELEN CLARK, PRIME MINISTER

New Zealand is renowned for the exploits and achievements of a long list of remarkable women.

Silvia Cartwright is soon to become New Zealand's second woman Governor-General. We have women holding the positions of Prime Minister, Attorney-General, Leader of the Opposition, Chief Justice, Cabinet Secretary, and chief executive of our biggest corporation. There are ten women ministers. In the arts, the work of Katherine Mansfield, Frances Hodgkins, Kiri Te Kanawa, Malvina Major and Keri Hulme are internationally celebrated. So are Susan Devoy and Erin Baker in the sports world.

This book provides an insight into the efforts required for women to achieve: the sheer hard work, the obstacles that must be overcome and the fulfilment that comes from attaining one's goals.

I count myself as lucky to be part of the post-war generation which came of age when women's abilities received more recognition. New Zealand women gained the right to vote in 1893, thanks to the efforts of Kate Sheppard and her fellow suffragists. But we waited until

1933 to see the first woman member of Parliament elected, Elizabeth McCombs. It wasn't until the 1970s that we saw women entering university in great numbers, and then entering the professions and achieving senior positions in the public and private sector. And it is only in recent years that women's achievements in sport have been taken more seriously.

My generation had opportunities that were not open to our mothers and grandmothers. We have been able to blaze a path for younger women to come along in much greater numbers. The diverse personalities in this book, many of them trailblazers, are an inspiration to us all.

Helen Clark

Helen Clark
Prime Minister

INTRODUCTION

This book is based on the belief that we are all capable of achieving wonderful things. Our dreams hold our hidden potential. They are the bridge between where we are now and where we would like to be. They call us to participate fully in life – to risk, to strive and to grow – and in so doing we discover the courage, strength and talents we need to live our lives out loud.

Twenty-two well-known women shared their experiences, personal philosophies and insights for this book. They are women who have passionately pursued what they love and as a result have achieved well. Most, through their dedication, have made a difference to the lives of many others.

Because the women in this book are outstanding women it is easy to fall into the trap of putting them on a pedestal and deciding they possess talents that enabled them to succeed where we cannot. In doing this we limit ourselves. We each have unique skills and talents we can develop and special things that capture our imagination. The size of our dream is not as important as the fact that it holds interest, possibilities and promise for us. Our own personal goals may be on a smaller scale than others but they are just as valid. The principles for achieving them are the same and are well illustrated by the personal experiences these women shared.

I consider myself blessed that the idea for this book came to me 'out of the blue' at a most unlikely time. The idea was accompanied by a rush of excitement and a sense of clarity and purpose – the feelings I associate with my intuition. Because it seemed like an inspired idea I decided I would pursue it and I'm grateful I chose that path. Writing this book has greatly enriched my life. Spending time with each of the women, hearing their stories, and at times witnessing their tears, has been inspiring and deeply moving. The wisdom they shared has given me invaluable insights into living life well – in a wholehearted, courageous, integral and generous way.

While the stories in this book are fascinating, thought-provoking and moving, it's important to remember that we too have a unique story which we are weaving every day of our life. It is never too late to weave in new, more vibrant threads – to do something different – to decide to pursue our special dream. The choice is ours.

At the end of her autobiography *Marching On* . . . Sonja Davies makes the comment: 'Nothing is ever too difficult to achieve. Only inertia can defeat us.' If there is one heartfelt message most of the women in this book wanted to convey it is that it is possible for people to achieve their dreams. Although these women faced challenges they have discovered when they hold true to their vision and keep moving forward they find within themselves the strength that ultimately leads to their achievements. This can be true for us too, if we commit wholeheartedly to our dreams.

I hope these stories will warm your heart, ignite your passion and encourage you in your endeavours. I wish you inspiration, success in your special pursuits and much pleasure on the journey.

Kay Douglas
2001

PURSUING DREAMS

. . . you can learn anything you need to learn to become anyone you want to become, to achieve anything you want to achieve. There are few limitations and most of them are on the inside, not on the outside.

Maximum Achievement, Brian Tracy

A dream is an ideal, aspiration or ambition that is dear to our heart. Our dreams are an expression of our true self, as unique as our fingerprints. They are reflections of our passion, talents, hopes and values and the particular purpose we are here to fulfil. Dreams come in all shapes and sizes: taking a special holiday; finding a job; buying a home; bringing about social change on a particular issue; becoming an adult student; creating a healthy lifestyle; going into business; being able to speak effectively to a group; leaving a destructive relationship; achieving at sports . . . the list is endless.

Achieving dreams is not just for 'other people' – the intelligent, talented, privileged or successful – it's for everyone. Pursuing our dreams gives our lives meaning and direction. We all need the sense of personal power we gain when we are moving ahead in our lives and the feeling of inner contentment that comes from having a life that is lived fully. Yet it can be a challenge to decide to follow our dreams. It requires courage to step away from an unsatisfactory job or relationship, to venture into unknown territory or to persevere when the going gets tough. When we do, the rewards are truly worth it. We are capable of achieving well if we give ourselves the chance.

Most of us have dreams we would love to achieve, yet how many of us expect to realise them? Rather than believing in our ability to achieve and perhaps even excel in the area that interests us, we can sell ourselves short by opting for the security and safety of our familiar routine. Too often we dismiss our dreams as impossible before even beginning to explore them. We make the mistake of focusing on the potential difficulties, rather than considering the possibilities. Dreams get put in the 'too hard' pile – forgotten, abandoned or written off as 'unrealistic'. Often the dreams we deny ourselves continue to niggle away at us in the years to come, bringing a sense of disappointment, frustration and regret. Eventually we may look back and sigh, 'If only . . .'

It can be difficult to contemplate our dreams if we are focused on day-to-day survival, but this is often the very time we need to have aspirations we are working towards. There are always choices we can make to improve our lives, even on a very small scale. An unhappy life, without a dream for change, becomes a life without hope. Our dreams can set us free from the most mundane and despairing of circumstances, provided we are willing to commit to them and take action. Over time small steps can lead to significant changes and sometimes inspiring achievements.

People who accomplish extraordinary things are ordinary people who have taken an area of interest and worked on it until they have achieved excellence. Just as successful people have chosen to take that path, we too can decide to put our energy and commitment into pursuing the things that hold special interest for us. Nothing worthwhile is ever achieved without effort. Undoubtedly it takes commitment, careful planning, hard work and perseverance to achieve our goals. However the effort required is not the drudgery of half-heartedly tackling a task we dislike. It is the inspired energy that comes from engaging in something we feel passionate about.

Passion is the driving force that provides the necessary impetus to pursue our dreams. There is a special power that comes when we follow our heart and do what we love, as the stories in this book show. Our real talents lie where our passion lies. Surprising and exciting opportunities often present themselves when we allow our passion to guide our choices. One of the biggest challenges people face is when they don't feel passionate or excited about the possibilities for their future. Fortunately passion can be discovered or rekindled and the questions in 'Personal Reflections' (pages 245–254) are designed to help you clarify where your passion lies. This section contains written exercises and questions to assist you to relate the contents of the thirteen themes in this book directly to your own life.

If an idea or dream lingers and seems to make sense to us at a deep level, we need to take that dream seriously, even if other people are unable to share our vision at that time. Many people have followed dreams they found compelling, which on the surface seemed impossible and have eventually succeeded. These people believed in what they were trying to achieve and were prepared to keep striving until they reached their goal. The stories shared by the women in this book reflect a similar conviction and courage. In many instances the women's commitment to their goals was so strong, that as they focused on achieving them, they were able to call on new reserves of energy and determination they didn't know they had.

It is possible for us all to find hidden reserves of energy and inspiration when we are engaged in a task that captures our imagination and ignites our passion. If we can take a chance and follow our heart's calling, we are likely to discover we will not only cope and survive, but we will thrive. Living life out loud is not about being reckless. It's about making the most of every day, breaking out of routine, taking calculated risks and daring ourselves to go beyond where we have been before. When we believe in ourselves, commit wholeheartedly to something that truly interests us, maintain our focus and give 100 per cent, we can create a fulfilling outcome, as Melissa Clark-Reynold's story shows.

Melissa Clark-Reynolds

'I believe that if we're spiritually, emotionally and intellectually
in alignment then boundless energy is going to follow.'

*Melissa is an inspiring entrepreneur who despite a
challenging childhood, becoming a solo parent at
18 and starting out in business without any assets,
achieved her goal to be a millionaire by the time
she was 35 years old. She is the founder and Managing Director of GMV Associates, an occupational
health and safety agency. She is also the General
Manager of Fusion, a private workplace insurer.
Melissa lives in Wellington with her baby daughter Grace and her 18-year-old son Rupert.*

*Having completed an honours degree in An-
thropology at Massey University when she was 19,
Melissa was disappointed to discover the practice
of anthropology, 'didn't really add any value to
the planet'. In 1987 she decided to retrain and completed a combined Masters
degree in public health and environmental planning at Rutgers University in New
Jersey, while working part time as a consultant and caring for her son. After returning to New Zealand in 1990, Melissa worked at The Ministry for the Environment,
then the Occupational Health and Safety section of the Department of Labour and
was the senior person on the team which wrote the Health and Safety in Employment Act.*

*Melissa's commitment to meaningful work led to her idea of creating GMV (an
acronym for Good Morning Vietnam) in 1992. Haunted by her childhood night-
mares of the mayhem of the Vietnam War, Melissa was determined to contribute
something positive to working conditions there. She approached the Business Development Board, Tradenz and Foreign Affairs in New Zealand with her idea to create
an occupational health and safety business in Vietnam as well as New Zealand, but
was told to forget it because it wouldn't work. Refusing to be put off, she contacted
the Hanoi Chamber of Commerce herself and received a positive response. Melissa's
vision and tenacity paid off and have continued to stand her in good stead as she
has gone on to bring her dream into reality.*

I decided in 1990 that I'd set up a business but I didn't know then what that business would be. I knew I didn't want to be self-employed anymore because the loneliness really got to me. I ended up getting a job for two years because I realised I wasn't a very good team player and I needed to learn that. I'm a really good team player now and I never want to be in a job where I'm on my own again. I believe we're meant to be part of a family unit or in teams of some sort and that's where I belong.

I knew that creating a business was going to be a challenge and I needed some practical skills. I didn't know how to read a cash flow or balance sheet or how to write a business plan, so in 1992 I decided to go to Hawaii and do a sixteen-day business course with Robert Kiyosaki. He has since written books and become a whole lot more famous. I learnt a massive amount there. It was basically a boot camp for entrepreneurs and it seemed a hell of a lot longer than sixteen days. It was really full on!

One of the tasks we had to do was to write a business plan. That's when I had my idea of creating a health and safety and environmental consultancy that worked in New Zealand and Vietnam. I was lying by the water, which I love, and I thought, 'Well, where have I always wanted to go and what do I want to do?' I decided to think big. I'd always wanted to go to Vietnam and I could see that right through my career I'd had this public health focus so I was well placed to do that.

Once I got the idea it was really important to me to have a plan, because even though I'm an ideas person I'm quite pragmatic. I like to know what the basic outline is and to have some structure around me. So I did a five-year plan with milestones and turnover targets and names of clients. I even named the staff I wanted. It was amazing because by the end of year three we had pretty much the kinds of people I was looking for and I even ended up with the clients that I'd written down at the time. I didn't even know anyone in them, but I just sat there in Hawaii and thought of the really big companies in New Zealand like Affco and ECNZ that it might be interesting to work with and I wrote them down.

That process was really important for two reasons. It made it seem more real and it chunked it down to actual milestones that were achievable. Just the thought of, 'Yes, I'm going to create a consultancy,' was too big. But to be able to say: 'I'm going to have three staff that do these things by this date; I'm going to have a partner in Vietnam by this date; I'm going to have a project in Vietnam by that date and I'm going to have these ten clients by the end of year one,' that was all doable so that made it much easier. The other thing that was good about it was that I could then actually measure it. At the end of six months, or a year, or three years I could look at the plan and say, 'Hey, I did that'. The cash flow might be scary but I'd done what I said I'd do and that's really important to me.

I presented my plan to the group and they were asked, 'Do you think she's going to do it?' and quite a few people said yes. I just remember thinking, 'You have no idea if I'm going to do this but you're humouring me. I am going to do this.' I really had the sense that these people in Hawaii, mostly Americans, couldn't figure out why this little blonde chick from New Zealand would want to go to Vietnam and do anything. I think even Robert thought I was crazy for the first few years. He'd catch up with me when he came to New Zealand and I'd say, 'Oh yeah, I'm still off to Vietnam,' and he'd just give me that 'in your dreams' look, like he didn't really believe it.

Naivety will take you a long way. If I'd known how hard it was going to be to set up my own business I might not have done it, but I do have this Pollyanna quality. I fundamentally believe it'll all be alright. I get into the depths of despair at times. There are times when I literally lie in bed with the covers over my head and won't get up that day, but fundamentally I think it will be OK so I keep going. And it has been a challenge! Sometimes we literally did eat porridge and pasta for weeks on end.

At 28 I wrote down that I'd be a millionaire by 35, and that seemed so big! I'd just started the business and it was, 'Right, this is what I'm going to do,' and part of that was needing to set myself a goal. It wasn't about the money. It was like challenging myself to prove that I could do it. Last year I got to the point where my net worth is more than one million and I thought, 'If I'd set it at ten million I could have done that too.'

For me it's been about constantly trying to stretch to do things I don't know how to do. I still remember taking my first cash flow down to the bank. I barely knew how to understand it myself, but it looked good and they seemed to understand it and they lent me the money on it, so I just kept doing it like that until I got it. I was literally in business three or four years before I knew how to read a balance sheet, but I produced them each year for the bank and for the accounts.

I know I wouldn't have started my business if I'd waited until I felt confident. I stepped into a void. I had these theoretical skills that I'd learned at the sixteen-day business school and I had what I believed was a good idea, but I was also a single mum with nothing and I was petrified that if something went wrong I'd lose everything. I thought if I went bankrupt that people would think I was a bad mother and I'd lose my child somehow. So I had a huge fear of failure that motivated me for a very long time. The other thing that really motivated me was my desire to provide for my child.

I was a mum a week after my eighteenth birthday and I was on my own with my son by the time I was 20, and I just had this huge drive to make sure we weren't poor. I think people discount poverty in New Zealand but it's very real. My mother was a single mother before the DPB and my father lived overseas and we regularly didn't have shoes to wear or enough to eat. My brother was known as the Biafran Boy. I was determined my child would never, ever experience that.

When it became obvious to me that I was driven by my fears of poverty and failure, I really had to stop and think about whether that was what I wanted to drive me. It's taken ten years of really solid work to not worry about money. I think what will drive me in the future is the competitiveness in me that says, 'Can you do it again? Was that a fluke? Prove it.' I'm also driven by a desire to give. I'm part of funding a medical clinic in Vietnam because it gives me pleasure to give back. I like to be inspired and I love working with other people and encouraging them to do things they don't think they're capable of.

When you're in the public eye people often say, 'Oh yeah, but they've always had it easy. What do they know?' and yet I went to speak at a school for single mothers in Porirua and we have these stories in common and we're not very different. I had a very difficult childhood. I grew up in a family that was quite violent and for me there was a lot of sexual violence as well. That has scarred me for life, physically as well as emotionally. At the time I knew what was happening wasn't OK but there wasn't anyone to talk to about it, because everyone around me seemed to be caught in the same web. I had a huge sense of responsibility towards my younger brother and I didn't want to leave him. I was also afraid of what might happen to my mother.

School was my safe place. I had a fantastic primary school teacher called Miss Gapper. She just encouraged me to dream and to read. I loved maths. I could literally spend hours in my bedroom making up long division for myself to do. It was a way of not thinking or feeling. It was perfect for me as a child, just to be in this very safe intellectual place.

I've done years of work on my healing. The more distance there is between me and my childhood, the more I can say that it really is in the past, but it does still affect who I am. I've found there were a whole lot of things that were emotionally hard for me to do, because as a child in that situation you set up particular ways of dealing with the world that are not very helpful as an adult.

One of the things I do have is courage and part of that courage is naming what happened. I think it's important that kids who are abused have some role models who are prepared to say, 'Yeah, this happened to me. Physically I have scars that will never leave my body, but it doesn't have to ruin my life.' We hear so often that kids who have been abused are going to go on to abuse their children and that really upsets me because I couldn't imagine hurting another human being. I think we have to have people who will stand up and say that's not necessarily true. I used to be worried that if I talked about my childhood abuse people would feel sorry for me and they'd discount me, but I've realised that's nothing to do with me. It's not my shame. I'm just how I am and that happened to me, so I can encourage other people that it's happened to.

The good side is that I do believe the worst things that could ever happen to me have already happened. No one will ever emotionally or physically hurt me again the way I was hurt. I'll never have the same depth of despair I had at times as a child. So that puts some perspective into the things that can go wrong as an adult. If I can survive all that, I can survive anything. Nothing can really damage me as a person now. Things might damage me physically but in the end that doesn't damage the actual me – the soul part of me. That understanding is a gift that gives me quite a lot of strength. Sometimes I get into a panic, then I stop and go, 'How bad is this going to be? How bad will going bankrupt be? Well it can't be as bad as anything that's already happened.'

My work in Vietnam has taught me to be grateful about the advantages I've had. When you drop yourself into a foreign culture and you don't know how to speak the language, people tend to relate to you for who you are. I've learnt a lot about my own ability to work with other people and that I do have something meaningful to contribute. The greatest challenge has been working with other foreigners up there and dealing with their cultural arrogance. Sometimes we'd work with Vietnamese people who had seven or eight languages at their fingertips and these arrogant New Zealanders would look down on them. It made me angry and it made me really want to learn the language and a lot more about Vietnam and its history. I think we have to be very careful about going to what we consider to be undeveloped countries and being arrogant about them. Just because people are poor it doesn't mean they're stupid.

In 1997 I did four months of really quite intensive Vietnamese language training at the University of Hanoi. I'd become exhausted and it was a sabbatical for me. I was well into burnout before I figured that I needed to take action. I'd done five years in the business. I'd written a five-year plan and I thought that at the end of five years I'd sell the company. When I started setting up the ACC side of the business I thought that by 1997 the government would have privatised ACC and I had this crushing sense of failure. I felt I'd done my five-year plan but the company wasn't in a state to be sold and I'd put all this money behind the government privatising ACC and they hadn't done it. I had a massive crisis of confidence and I thought, 'I'm all wrong. This business is going to fail and I'm going to be stuck in it forever,' and I began to resent it. I felt like I'd created a job for myself instead of a real company. I knew if I didn't get some space I was going to crash and burn because I'd got to a point where I had nothing left to give anybody. I needed to go away and be me and not be the business.

When I decided to go there probably were people who thought I was crazy, but they've always thought I was crazy. Saying you were going to set up a consultancy in Vietnam in 1992 or a private ACC company in 1994 was crazy. So I got used to people thinking I was crazy and I just thought, 'That's their problem. I'm going to do this.'

Taking the time off in Vietnam was fantastic. It refreshed me and gave me the opportunity to get some real distance. I thoroughly enjoyed being a student. I was riding my motorbike around as well and I also worked to set up things at the clinic I'm involved in. While I was there I decided that I'd earn my keep so I played games with myself. I taught English in this funny little backstreet school for $5 an hour. All I had to do was to teach five hours a week and that paid for all of my food, but it meant I was on a $25 a week budget, so I had to eat on the street and that meant I had to speak Vietnamese better. I rented out a room with a Vietnamese family in a Vietnamese neighbourhood, with no other foreigners around. I took my motorbike away on holiday and I went to this Vietnamese beach resort because that's all I could afford and I had a fantastic time. I had to learn how to get my motorbike repaired in Vietnamese. So it all tied together and I found if I put myself in that situation I could do it.

That experience taught me I could always start again. I could have probably got myself a consulting job for US$150 an hour but I didn't want to do that. I wanted to prove to myself that I could survive, and that's made me much more confident. It made me feel like I could walk into a new country and I could make friends, find a job, support myself and it would all be alright. My story about my childhood or my story about my success as a businessperson was all irrelevant. When you meet brand new people in a brand new language you have to go to shorthand and it's how you interact with them that matters, not who you've ever been in terms of any story about yourself. That was really good for me.

When I came back to New Zealand in October 1997 I said, 'They're going to privatise ACC. It's just a matter now of really making this happen.' Then I literally put my head down and cranked and by July 1998 it was in the budget and the government had announced that it was happening.

Even though I've achieved a lot it's only recently I've felt like I really know what I'm doing because Fusion is such a big company. We did 160 million dollars turnover in the first nine weeks. It made me feel much more confident leading a team of a couple of hundred staff and knowing that they did a good job and that we made money and the people liked working there and I liked the people I worked with. I realised that in the industry I was seen as a leader and in the private ACC market nobody has been in it as long as I have.

I used to do a lot of public speaking about technical subjects and I can do that in my sleep but lately I've started speaking about myself and sometimes I've not slept the night before. It's that sense of being exposed, of standing up and saying, 'This is who I am and this is what I think.' There's a voice inside me that says, 'Who cares what you think? Who are you to even have all these thoughts?' So I just get up and do it anyway and look confident. I say to myself, 'act casual'. I know if I pretend that I'm at home with this I'm more likely to be OK. And I get through and I think, 'Wow, they thought that was really good,' or, 'That wasn't so hard,' or, 'I only botched that up a little in the middle and no one seemed to notice.' That's how my confidence has grown.

I believe my life is a work in progress, so that means learning all the time and correcting all the time. I don't believe that any of us are perfect. Having courage is really important to me, that sense of stepping off the cliff and knowing I'm going to be alright. I don't think I'm a risk taker. I like to have a plan and a team around me. I like to do something I think is challenging but I don't think that's risky because if it's looking like it isn't going to work I'll try something else. I'm not the least bit reckless.

I like the challenge of setting up companies; of creating something out of nothing. I know if I lost everything I've got such good skills that I'd start again in a heartbeat.

I like to be able to set goals and measure them. That gives me a sense of satisfaction. I've learnt not to care what other people think and not to want to achieve their goals. I think that you can't be an entrepreneur and not work hard. I've always wanted to build something that went on and survived without me and I think that takes hard work.

Over the years my friends have often given me a hard time about working so hard, but I do what I love and there's amazing energy that comes from doing something you think is meaningful and useful. Some people say, 'How can being in insurance be meaningful and useful?' I don't see Fusion as being 'in insurance'. It's in the business of keeping New Zealanders alive. We prevent people from getting killed at work and if they get injured we work with them to get them back to productive lives as quickly as possible. That's meaningful to me.

Even though I might be physically tired at times, my work inspires me and interests me. Although I haven't worked weekends in years, before my daughter was born I'd do a twelve-hour day three or four times a week. One of the reasons for that was for the first five or six hours a day I wanted to see the people I worked with. With a couple of hundred staff, that's a lot of people to get around regularly. I liked to stop and have coffee and chat with people and see what was actually happening. That meant I had to write or read in the evening when it was quiet. Sometime I wish I'd had more time to spend with my son in the last few years, but I also know that you can't have everything. We get on well and he's a great guy and I've done my best.

I feel spiritual about my work in the sense that I believe I'm doing my life's purpose. It's like a vocation I've been called to do and this is how I chose to spend my life. I believe that if we're spiritually, emotionally and intellectually in alignment, boundless energy is going to follow. The money comes because I'm doing the right thing.

I believe in a higher power and I believe in a respect for other human beings, partly because of the fact that they're human beings and partly because of the higher power in them. As a child I used to lie in bed and talk to God and that gave me a sense of not being on my own and that was important for me. Even when I'm in pretty deep despair I have a sense of being in someone's care and that there will be a gift in there – something to learn.

Going somewhere like Vietnam gives me a stronger sense of spirituality because I see a country that has been ravaged by destruction and death and war for 600 years and yet people have a strong sense of themselves, respect for one another and compassion and I think that comes from a higher power. It's not just that they're human qualities, they're touching the divine.

Melissa's message

A piece of advice I'd give is when in doubt act as if you know what to do. If I'd waited until I knew how to do things I wouldn't have done them. Robert Kiyosaki told me, 'Fake it till you make it,' and that's a great phrase. I think if you act confidently, it's easier to feel confident.

If you don't love your dreams nobody's going to, so if you have a dream that compels you I think you owe it to yourself to give it a go. When I started out I didn't have anything – literally nothing – except some debt. I didn't even have a credit card. I'd much rather have given it a go and found that it didn't work than to have regretted not doing it. I think that it's never too late to start and there never is a right time to do anything — to have a baby or to start a business, whatever — so if you have a sense of vocation you may as well just get on with it. You need people round you to help you but in the end it has to be your desire to do it.

BELIEVING

Beliefs help us tap the richest resources deep within us, creating and directing these resources in the support of our desired outcomes.

Unlimited Power, Anthony Robbins

The power of belief accomplishes marvellous things. Belief in a positive outcome is the driving force for people who achieve their dreams. One of the most deciding factors about whether or not we will succeed in our endeavours is the quality of our beliefs; in order to succeed we need to believe in ourselves and our dreams. Our beliefs limit or liberate us. If we approach our dream halfheartedly, believing in the possibility or probability of failure, we are setting the wheels in motion for just that outcome. In contrast, when we fully expect a positive outcome we draw to ourselves the resources we need to help us progress. We may not know exactly how we are going to reach our desired outcome but when we are of the firm opinion that we will, we generate the skills and energy required to do so.

Some people are fortunate to have grown up being consistently affirmed and encouraged. They pursue their dreams from a position of high self-esteem, trust in the world as an abundant place and expectations of having a safe, happy, rewarding life. Those of us who haven't had this experience, or who have encountered significant disappointments and hurts along the way, often need to actively work to develop positive beliefs in our own worth and ability. By holding on to old beliefs from the past that are not serving us we don't see the opportunities that are in front of us. We limit our ability to bring new, exciting people and satisfying situations into our lives. If we find it difficult to envisage the future positively this is an indication that we need to spend time consciously working on improving the quality of our beliefs.

Believing

We each have the power to change what we think. We can decide to break old negative habits – to think uplifting thoughts rather than depressing ones; to focus on problem solving rather than complaining; to let go of the things that are holding us back; to stop worrying unnecessarily and to dwell on what we wish to accomplish rather than potential obstacles. In essence we can decide to develop a pattern of optimism – the expectation that good will prevail. Optimism promotes confidence, happiness, passion and success. When we see our dreams in a positive light we approach situations wholeheartedly and our enthusiasm captures other people's imagination and opens doors.

If we are prone to negative thinking it can take time to break this destructive habit but it is well worth the effort. Self-awareness is power. At any time we can tune into our thoughts and ask: Is this way of thinking helping or hindering my progress towards my dream? If our thoughts are bringing us down we can choose to change them. The spoken word is a very powerful means of changing beliefs. We can develop positive beliefs by repeatedly affirming what we want in short, positive, present tense statements.

Our self-image is pivotal to the success or failure of our endeavours. Whether we believe ourselves to be competent and talented or inadequate and undeserving of success we are likely to act accordingly. We have the power to develop our self-image as we choose by deliberately focusing on our strengths or those characteristics we would like to develop. The more we can incorporate such attributes as determination, tenacity, focus, commitment and courage into our self-image, the more we will foster a positive belief in ourselves that will empower us to act boldly. We can consciously utilise our past successes to boost our self-esteem by recording them in a journal or repeatedly visualising them. Each success we have, no matter how small, helps to instil a belief in our personal power and ability to create what we desire.

Every dream happens first in our mind. We can help to bring our dreams into reality by actively imagining them as if they are already achieved. This mental dress rehearsal paves the way for the real event, as several of the stories in this book illustrate. The more vivid the impressions of our success in our mind, the more our sense of positive anticipation grows and the easier we can bring our dreams into reality. The following stories shared by Sonja Davies and Theresa Gattung highlight the importance of having a positive self-image and demonstrate that having an optimistic outlook can have powerful results.

Sonja Davies

'I think it's true that if you really believe you're going to be alright you will be!'

The fact that Sonja was voted Woman of the Century in the New Zealand Women's Weekly *reader's poll is a reflection of the courage and commitment with which she lives. Sonja has faced numerous life challenges, yet has continued to live life to the full and work towards creating a better society — a vision she is passionate about.*

Sonja was born illegitimately in 1923. She was brought up by foster parents and her grandparents for her first seven years before living with her mother and stepfather. She was married briefly and unhappily at 17, then in 1941 she fell in love with Red Brinsen, an American serviceman. A few months after their daughter Penny was born, he went missing in action. Sonja contracted tuberculosis as a nurse and became dangerously ill, spending years in hospital separated from her daughter. In 1946 Sonja married an old friend, Charlie Davies. She was widowed in 1970. Her son Mark died tragically in an accident in 1978 and her daughter died in 1994 of motor neurone disease.

Sonja has had a long trade union and political career. She was the first woman elected to the Federation of Labour executive and the first to become FOL vice president. She was a Labour MP from 1987 until 1993, and is a member of the exclusive Order of New Zealand. Sonja has written two inspiring autobiographies: Bread and Roses *and* Marching On.... *She lives in Masterton and continues to be actively involved in the issues she cares deeply about.*

I'm somebody who's 76 and feels 18 inside. I still feel that I've got a lot to do but I'm not physically able to do a lot of things because of the tuberculosis that I had. I've only got half a lung working, and have had for many years, and that's compounding as I get older and I've had a fall and that has shaken me a bit. But I'm fine, everyone's very pleased with me and the way I've gotten over it.

I was politically aware very young in my life and I've always believed passionately that if things were wrong for people you had to do what you could to put them right – to help people. I've just seen things that needed to be done and found the best way to do them if I could. You don't always succeed, but a lot of the time you do and that makes it worthwhile. I believe we need to get people back to trusting each other and relying on each other and working together in community initiatives and joint ventures – people working together for the good of everybody.

That vision began for me when I was about 8 years old. I was driving along with my mother in the tram car and I saw all the Dunedin windows boarded up because they had been shattered and I said, 'What happened there?' She said, 'It's the unemployed, they're lazy. They don't want to work.' I said, 'I don't believe you.' That was the first time I'd ever said that to her. 'People would work if they had jobs. There aren't jobs Mother. You know that.' I can also remember at about the same age going with my mother to visit a new mother to give her some clothes for her baby because her husband was unemployed. Later my mother said to me, 'She wasn't very grateful.' I said, 'Why should she be grateful? Did you do it just to have somebody be grateful?' So I think my social conscience has always been there.

I'd spent most of the first seven years of my life living with my grandparents. They taught me to love books and reading and poetry. And they taught me that I was very important, but I wasn't more important than anyone else and that I should have a sense of responsibility towards other people and respect their property. So I grew up knowing all those things and believing that I could do anything I wanted to do.

My mother got me back to live with her and my stepfather and my baby stepsister when she remarried. My stepfather really didn't want me there. He poured all his love into his daughter and just didn't like me at all so he put me down all the time. It was difficult for my mother because she loved him. My grandmother often said, 'We should never have let you go back. We should have just said no she's staying with us.' Fortunately the things that my grandparents taught me were a sort of buffer so I knew I wasn't useless and I wasn't senseless and I could do things, and that just made me more determined to do them.

I was no good at maths and my stepfather was a whiz at maths and he used to tell me I was stupid because I couldn't do it. When I finally went to Dunedin North Intermediate I had a wonderful, inspirational teacher called Miles Botting and he said to me, 'Look it doesn't matter that you can't do maths. You probably won't need it. You're not going into science. You're wonderful at English, history, geography, art, music and sport so that's fine. Just do well in those things.' So that was great.

As a teenager I was very rebellious. My stepfather was very conservative and militaristic and I was a pacifist at that stage and he said all pacifists should be put up against a wall and shot. I really became quite demoralised. When I was 14 we went to live in Auckland and I couldn't get into a secondary school at that stage because they were all full. The only one which could take me said I had to go back to the third form and I was just about to go into the fifth so I refused to do that and went out and got myself a job at a lending library. I missed the companionship of my peers, so I'd go home with a pile of books every weekend and just read and read.

I'd always wanted to be a nurse and I embarked on this as soon as I could. During this time I got tuberculosis and I was really very ill. I had to go into hospital and I couldn't have any contact with my baby daughter because it's infectious. I was in hospital for altogether ten years. That was a very hard and lonely time. I read an awful lot. There was a time when I just slept and slept and slept. I had hardly any weight at all and I was desperately ill but I thought, 'No, I'm going to survive.' Even when I was haemorrhaging all over the place and the staff were horrified, I didn't believe I was going to die because my grandmother told me I wasn't going to. She was a clairvoyant and she rang me the day I went into hospital and said, 'You are in great danger and you are going to be desperately ill but you will not die. Remember that! There's a lot of things you're going to do yet.' So I told the nurses, 'Don't worry, I'll be alright.' I really believed that. Three months later my doctor came back from England he said, 'I hear you've been spitting a bit of blood. That's good. That would have gotten rid of a lot of rubbish off your chest.' That put it all into perspective! He told me he'd brought me back a new drug that was going to fix me. And it did!

Since then I've been incredibly well, but as I've got older if I've got a cold or the flu I've got pneumonia – other than that I've been fine. Yet the doctors told me by the time I was 45 I wouldn't be able to walk at all because of my lung capacity. When they said that I thought, 'I don't believe you.' Since I was 42 I've walked all around Siberia and America and Canada. I think it's true that if you really believe that you're going to be alright you will be! I think a lot of psychosomatic illnesses are because people don't believe that. They haven't had anybody to give them that feeling. I think that's the greatest gift my grandmother gave me.

It's like recently I had a lung haemorrhage and I was rushed into hospital and there was a visiting American doctor there. After I'd had my x-ray he said, 'I think you've got lung cancer', and I said, 'Don't be ridiculous. I can't fit that in! I haven't got time in my life for that.' I wasn't going to take that on board. Not for a minute. He said, 'Well, you'll have to go down to Wellington Hospital and get them to examine you.'

I knew the doctor who was going to do the examination and before I went to theatre he said, 'Whatever it is Sonja, when you come round I'll tell you.' When I came to my two six-foot-eight grandsons were on either side of me and my friend Mary was there and a couple of others and I said, 'Do you people know something I don't?' And they said, 'No, we haven't talked to the doctor.' And he came up and said, 'It's fine. It was a capillary and when you had pneumonia you coughed and burst it.' When I came back to Masterton I was pleased to tell that other doctor that I was perfectly alright.

I've lost quite a lot of major people in my life so I've certainly been tempered. I think when my husband died I was expecting it because he'd already had two major heart attacks. But it was still devastating. And then when my son Mark was killed suddenly in the Turangi tunnel that was a terrible thing, and I never really got over that. I didn't realise until he died how many other people that I didn't know loved him very much and how helpful he'd been to them. For two years I was just angry and then I started remembering all the wonderful times I'd had with him and what a lovely boy he was. He was just great.

And then when my daughter died I had five years to say goodbye to her because she died of motor neurone disease. That was a very, very draining, searing time. She was such a wonderful teacher and she was so intelligent and was loved by her children and her pupils and she loved them. She had just won a scholarship and was going to spend the next year in Auckland at the university. When she found out about her illness she was told in a horrible way by this overseas doctor, 'Oh, you've got motor neurone disease and you're going to die. There's nothing anybody can do for you.' They still aren't very good at it. They've got to learn. And then when my best friend Con died of cancer, that was pretty terrible too.

Friends have helped me through these times. My friends have always been wonderful to me — always been supportive and done marvellous things for me. You feel you'd be churlish not to appreciate that. Really I basically got through by thinking, 'Well, I've just got to go on.' You do start to wonder. Why me? What terrible thing have I done that these things should go on happening? But, it's useless to think like that. It's very easy to go right down and find it hard to come up again. I was very anxious not to do that. I stopped myself by keeping busy. When Mark died I had a very demanding job, I was vice president of the Federation of Labour and I was travelling all over the place and speaking and working and holding meetings and I didn't have time to think of myself. That was the big thing!

I've always been passionate about the things I've been involved with over the years. I cared deeply about the preschool movement and worked very hard for that for fourteen years. Then in the Trade Union Movement I felt passionately about people who were being exploited. I was the only woman on the FOL and the only woman vice president. Of course in Nelson when I was on the Hospital Board in 1956 I was the only woman and then on the City Council there were only two of us. I didn't mind. I thought, 'If they're not going to make a fuss about it neither am I', and when they saw that I wasn't just a little lady who was going to make the tea and bring the sandwiches, they treated me like an ordinary person. But things happened. When I wanted to sit on the bench when I was a JP they told me I couldn't because no lady had ever wanted to. I said, 'Well maybe I'm no lady, but I want to.'

Then I topped the poll at the City Council and it was customary for the person who topped the poll to be the Chair of the Works Committee. And the mayor rang me up and said, 'Look, the fellows wouldn't stand for it', and I said, 'Well, they'll just have to sit down won't they?' and he said, 'Look, I can't do it. It'll cause a terrible row.' So he made me Chair of the Electricity Committee and the Gas Committee instead. When I went to the Electricity Conference I was the only woman delegate. It was a bit lonely. Some of the men were very patronising, some thought they could get me into bed and others just treated me normally.

Change happens slowly. Things sometimes take twenty years to achieve. I often think, 'Now here they are doing this or that as if it's normal and I had to fight for it.' I think I was lucky in a way to go through all the struggles because I realised what prejudices there were and knew how to fight them. I used to say to myself, 'Do I really believe in this and is it worth fighting for?' and if I thought it was I'd just get on with it. Of course I'm retired now but there's still lots of things I'm involved in. I'm always busy.

It's very frustrating being slowed down by my fall. It happened when I was feeding the chooks and the ducks. The ducks were nibbling my new pantyhose so I went to kick them out of the way and I slipped and fell and crack! I didn't know I'd broken my hip and leg but it was excruciating. I had to crawl inside and I passed out and came round about half an hour later and couldn't get to the telephone. I dragged myself into the bedroom somehow and it took me ages to get up on the bed. I just thought if I could get into bed I'd be alright and when I woke up in the morning I'd probably be sore but I'd be OK and I'd just rub it with some arnica. But it wasn't an arnica situation! I had a very fitful night's sleep and I was in a lot of pain but I still couldn't get to the telephone by the bed. My cat Abby knows I don't like her sitting on the telephone, but I said to her, 'Go and sit on the phone Abby' and she looked at me and I said it again and she went and sat on it. I told her to knock the receiver off and she did and I just grabbed it and rang a neighbour.

I had to have a dreadful operation without any general anaesthetic because of my lungs, so I could hear chipping and sawing and chopping. The orthopaedic surgeon was really wonderful but it was a terrible experience. And then the next day they got me up because they don't put you into plaster anymore. It was unbearable but they had to do it, that's part of the treatment. I'm coming right now and they've given me a wonderful walker which I use when I go out and walk round the garden or feed the chooks. Really you've just got to get on with it and not dwell on things.

I've always been very lucky with the doctors I've had and the staff who have looked after me. That's why I'm so passionate about saving Masterton Hospital and keeping a quality state funded health service available to everybody. This whole idea of hospitals having to make a profit is just anathema to me because hospitals are not businesses, they're service centres and they're there to give quality care for whoever needs it regardless of their age, sex or race. The doctors and the nurses who do the caring have got to be cared about as well. Masterton Hospital is a lovely hospital and it's run down. That's something I feel really strongly about.

Sonja's message

Self-esteem is one of the vital ingredients for really achieving the things you want to. You can't do anything if you haven't got any faith in yourself and if you don't really like yourself. So I'd say start with yourself and build yourself up and go from there. If you've got things that you want to achieve and you feel too afraid to follow them then perhaps you need counselling to help you with your self-esteem. There's plenty of people around who can help you. Go out and talk to them.

When I look out and see the wonderful clouds in the sky I think, 'There's just so much that's wonderful in this world but so many people are suffering.' I think we're really very privileged to be able to live in this country and breathe this air, but things can be better. So really it's not just about doing things for ourselves but doing things to help other people as well, keeping up the community spirit.

Theresa Gattung

'I believe that you envisage first and then you bring into being that which you've envisaged.'

Theresa is the CEO of New Zealand's largest com-
pany, Telecom. Her phenomenal success at reaching
this position at only 37 is a reflection of the deter-
mination and dedication with which she has pursued
her goals. From a young age Theresa had her sights
set firmly on success. Theresa was so committed to
her goal of becoming a CEO, she wore suits to uni-
versity to mentally prepare herself for the role.

The oldest in a family of four girls, Theresa was
born in Wellington in 1962. Her parents had emi-
grated from Britain with the intention of giving
their children a good start in life. From the age of
11, Theresa attended McKillop College, a small,
private Catholic girls' school in Rotorua. Before she
left at age 17, she studied every available subject in the 6th and 7th form except
physics.

In 1983 Theresa completed a Bachelor of Management Studies (Hons.) at Waikato
University. Over the next four years she went on to study law and completed a law
degree while working part time for the first year, then full time after being pro-
moted to market research manager for TVNZ. Theresa chose not to practise law but
instead joined National Mutual where she became marketing manager. When she
was 28 Theresa became chief manager of marketing for the BNZ. After four years
she moved into Telecom's top marketing job, became group general manager, services,
in 1996 and was promoted to CEO in 1999. Theresa lives with her partner John
Savage in Wellington.

I've always admired women who live very self-determined lives and who've really been clear about what they thought their contribution to the world was and then organised life to support them in doing that. I'd be surprised if I didn't have one of the biggest libraries of books on how women succeed because I've collected them for a very long time.

My definition of a successful person is someone who understands themselves really well, who is comfortable with the situation they find themselves in, who deals well with life's adversities and who doesn't end up thinking they know everything. Someone who remains open to advice, coaching and new directions but who has a real sense of living a self-determined life. That's what I wish for everyone, but particularly for women because when you read a lot of feminist literature about women not having their own voice, what it comes down to is they didn't lead self-determined lives. They were restricted either by societal norms or those around them.

I think being committed to your relationships and to what you're trying to achieve in the world is a source of deep contentment. I'd say I'm motivated to be the best that I can be. For me it's always been about nurturing the talents I was born with, making the best use of them and seeing where that took me. I've wanted to go as far as I could, to see what my limits were in terms of what I could achieve — and to stay sane at the same time. I've always been quite focused and determined and thought about what I was trying to create. I believe that you envisage first and then you bring into being that which you've envisaged.

I'm never down for very long and if I was in a situation that wasn't tenable, where I couldn't be optimistic, I'd actually move away. I can't stay in the space of being down or feeling that life is a real struggle. It just doesn't feel natural to me. Occasionally I've been in that situation and I'll either change my attitude or change the situation. I won't stay where I feel that I'm a victim or that I've got no choice.

I was the eldest daughter of immigrant parents who came from a working-class background and really wanted to succeed. I was very much loved and supported by my parents and was very lucky to have a father who truly believed that girls could do anything. Being the eldest I was expected to lead the way and so I was really encouraged to achieve from a very early age.

With the influence of my family I formed the view, at a very young age, that economic independence was really important for a woman. I saw that you could not determine your own life if you were dependent on a man to support you financially. I always thought that I'd work in a reasonably highly paid occupation and support myself and be able to travel and enjoy life.

When I was about 12 I had the Goethe quote 'Boldness has genius, power and magic' on my wall along with my David Bowie posters. I kept that quote on my wall for years even though it got really tatty because I'd move it around when I'd repaint my room. That is part of a much bigger quote about living a self-determined life. The beauty about the complete Goethe quote is that it says once you've made a commitment and embarked on a path, all manner of things will rearrange themselves to support you which you could never have foreseen.

I had strong female role models about leadership and living a good life and going for it from my private Catholic girls' school. I never saw discrimination until I was 17 when I was in mixed classes with the local Catholic boys' school and there was the assumption on the part of one of the teachers that the girls wouldn't be as good at maths as the boys. I was puzzled by that discrimination but it didn't impact on my view of life one iota, because by then I knew deep down that men and women were equal because that's how I'd been brought up. That was about the time I started reading more feminist literature and realising there were structural barriers to women succeeding. I guess that just really reinforced my view about the need for personal independence and the need to have relationships that weren't bound by stereotypes – that gave you the space to be who you were.

For me the Catholic faith wasn't about restrictions. I did get the messages that women couldn't be priests at a superficial level but they never really penetrated the core of my being, because I had this deep sense that anything and everything was possible. We had to live life with good intent, in a way that was true for us. There would always be guides in the form of people who would help us see what was right for us and we should remain open to that. Ultimately it was our responsibility how our life turned out and we could determine that. I've always believed that.

At the age of 17 I decided one of my life goals was to run a public company in New Zealand by the time I was 40, and I also saw having a happy, stable, loving relationship as a life goal. I split up with a boy-friend in my teenage years and was really heartbroken so I got quite analytical about the sort of person I'd choose for my life partner. It's not a coincidence that John and I have a very happy relationship. I could see back then that I needed someone like him. So my two main goals have played out exactly.

About that time I decided to start a clipping file about women who had succeeded around the world, but particularly in New Zealand and Australia. I've still got that file and I still put things into it, although not as much as I used to. That was all about envisaging the future I wanted and then bringing it into being. By cutting those articles out and putting them in a file and relooking at them I was able to bring some of those women into my life. For example I kept a lot of clippings about Sharon Lord when she was visiting New Zealand running seminars about equal employment opportunities. I had the thought deep down, 'I'd like to meet this woman,' and I met her un-expectedly in the US a few years later and she's been a friend and mentor ever since.

I had a very tough time in a physical sense in my mid-twenties when I had temporomandibular joint syndrome, which manifested as constant toothache. It went undiagnosed for many months. Psychia-trists were telling me it was all in my head and I had several teeth root filled, which turned out to be unnecessary. It took quite a while to come right but I tend to be optimistic and even in my darkest hours of being in agony it never occurred to me that I wouldn't find what the problem was and treat it and be right as rain. I did learn from that time because that's when I started swimming every day and having regular massages and taking regular breaks and stopped drinking tea and coffee and those things have helped me keep my stress down over the years.

I do think that the idea of balance is really important and I try to remain in tune with what's going on for me spiritually and what my body's telling me through physical manifestations. I exercise every day and keep physically fit. I quite like my own company and enjoy reading, horse riding, swimming, walking and exploring things. I spend my working life with people so my leisure time tends to just be me, or John and myself. I get up early every morning so I can swim and I love having long luxurious baths most days. That sort of activity is also a form of contemplation.

A self-determined life for me includes time out for reflection. I have to tell myself to slow down and not to rush through things. It's important to be able to reflect and review what's happening and be prepared to be flexible as opportunities arise; to remain creative and curious and to see where the next stage of my life might go and not to be so rigid about what my goals are that I become closed to other things. I try to structure enough rest and quiet time and I know when I need space to reflect because I'm not able to digest all the experiences that are happening and integrate them. It's also quite important for me to incorporate other people's ideas and advice into my own sense of judgement and I need time to do that as well. If I'm getting too much input I can't bring it together.

I think that making time for a spiritual component in one's life through reading, prayer or meditation is so important, just trying to be open to what's really going on for you. If you live a very hectic life you can really shut that down. I do believe that the material world is not all there is. I'm no longer a practicing Catholic but I try to have a prayerful approach in terms of being open to what messages I'm being sent and I believe quite strongly that when this job is over the next thing will emerge and I'll still be Theresa without the power and the trappings. I do think that getting in touch with what I'm here to achieve has played a part in my success. This job will remain in place for as long as it's the right thing and then something else will happen.

We're not here by accident; we're all here for a reason and we can each make a huge difference. We're a particular combination of skills and talents and we're supposed to use that, both to actualise ourselves and for the good of everyone else around us. We're all on a different path and we're supposed to be open to learning from each other. A self-determined life to me does not mean a selfish life because no one is going to be happy if they aren't linked in with their wider community.

I believe that people create their own destiny and each of us has that opportunity and responsibility. If we put out good intentions and we want to make a positive difference, that's what we'll do. If we put out that we want to live a shy, frightened, underachieving life, that's exactly what will happen. That's been my experience of the way the world operates. I wasn't born with a silver spoon in my mouth. We choose what reality we create by the set of possibilities we hold for ourselves. Whether we say, 'That's the way it is and there's nothing I can do about it. I can't succeed because I'm a female or Maori or born in New Zealand or born on Stewart Island,' or whether we face the facts as they are and say, 'Discrimination does exist. There are structural barriers. Some people have had a better start than others, but I can shape my life to be however I want it to be.' That fits with what I feel comfortable believing because it allows for a greater force at work than us, but it allows for us to be a key player in what happens in our lives.

I think courage is really important for everyone, but particularly for women because we're often held back by our fears – the fear of failure, fear of success, fear of stepping outside the box we've put ourselves in or we think the world has put us in. I had a very fortunate childhood but even in the most fortunate of lives you get told that you can't do things. I think it does take courage to live a self-determined life because there are always going to be people who want you to play a particular script in their lives. We are the director and actor in our own lives so we need to say, 'This is my script and this is the way I'm playing it.' We are offered opportunities all the time and we choose whether or not to respond to them. It's really important to overcome that 'I feel a fool' factor and, 'I couldn't possibly do that,' and that's about boldness. It's about saying that one can create what one wants. If we respond with courage more opportunities will unfold.

The world is full of people who say things can't be done. I'm sure that if I articulated my goal to run a large company before I was 40 to anyone except my nearest and dearest they'd have said, 'It simply can't be done!' At times it's been important to protect myself from that by keeping my goals to myself, but at the end of the day it doesn't matter what other people think. What matters is what's in your head and acknowledging that fear of failure and success and change is a human thing.

I was told many times in my career that I couldn't stay in marketing and become a CEO. I had to change direction. I was also told many times that I couldn't stay in New Zealand if I wanted to run a big company. I had to go overseas and get work experience offshore. But that was not my script. I loved living in this country and I loved what I was doing and I believed that if I did what I loved I had much more chance of being promoted than if I moved sideways to do something else, even though the story was that you had to do that to get ahead.

I've tried to keep open to opportunities that are being presented to me all the time. Every time I've changed jobs I've changed industries and I've left a situation where I felt quite comfortable. Each time that's taken a degree of courage but I know if I want to lead an evolving life I can't stay still. I've never switched jobs because a head-hunter has chased me. I've done it the hard way, by phoning or answering ads. I've had a vision of where I wanted to go and I've squashed down my fear enough to say, 'Right I'm going to take the next step. What's the worst that can happen? Rejection, and then I'll go on to another path.'

When I was thinking about leaving the BNZ and going to Telecom it was a big leap and I had to take my courage in my hands and make a jump into the unknown. The way I did that was to ring and say, 'Here I am!' I'd agonised for ages about ringing Telecom and saying, 'Look, I think that I can do the marketing job.' I put it off because I was scared. Finally one day I just thought, 'I've got to do it today,' and I rang and got put through to the head of human resources and it was the day that he was about ready to meet with someone else. That was definitely the universe telling me through my intuition, 'Do it today.' I've got better over time at acknowledging those little signals and listening to them.

I've definitely noticed as I've got older that I've got more intuitive about the right things to do. Sometimes I just wake up in the middle of the night and think, 'Oh yes, that's what was going on there.' Sometimes it takes a couple of times before the message gets through, but I know if something keeps coming up I should act on it. One of the issues for me now is, how do I live a life where I have enough time to pay attention to those signals? That's where I need to allow time for reflection.

I don't think I've got to where I am simply because I knew what to do and when to do it. I've had so much timely support and interventions and wisdom from other people and a few fantastic mentors, most recently Roderick Deane. I've been very fortunate to have the unstinting support of John and Chris, my personal assistant. And I've benefited by the sacrifices and the struggles of the women who've gone before. I don't think we should take for granted the things that we've got today as women. I have those people to thank for the fact that the environment I find myself in at this point in history is as it is.

Theresa's message

If we don't do that which we feel called to do, we know in our inner soul that we failed ourselves in terms of living a rich life. I do believe that whatever situation you find yourself in, it's never too late to reinvent yourself. The only person holding you back is you. There are structural barriers but they're not insurmountable. Whatever issues you're facing, life starts today. If you feel in a really stuck situation then it helps to draw on your inner strength and have the courage to say, 'I've got to put myself in a different space.' You can move forward from there. It's up to each of us.

I've always intuitively believed that when we're bold about what we conceive of, it's going to come back to us one thousandfold. I think if you're being true to yourself you will be supported in all sorts of unexpected ways. I absolutely believe that you have to look the part before you become the part and you have to envisage yourself in a happy relationship or job before you can bring that into being. If you're committed and believe your goal is possible you will be able to bring it about. Ultimately our life will be how we write the script.

CREATING A VISION

Through imagination we can visualise the uncreated worlds of the potential that lie within us.

The 7 Habits of Highly Effective People, Stephen Covey

Our lives are far too precious to be left to just slip away, lost to mind-numbing routine, compromise or coping. We are all here to learn, grow and express ourselves in our own unique way. A few people do this in ways that impact positively on the lives of many, but for most of us our contributions are far more humble. Nevertheless our dreams are important. They express our heart's desire and achieving them can energise, excite and satisfy us as nothing else can.

Each of us has a life purpose – a particular underlying aspiration that is present in the activities that bring us our deepest sense of fulfilment and joy. If we take the time to clarify our purpose, we gain a wonderful foundation from which to create a balanced and inspiring vision for our life. The idea of discovering our purpose can sound much grander (and more difficult) than it is. It involves thinking about our most satisfying achievements and looking for the common themes. If you are not already clear about your life purpose the questions on page 247 will help you to clarify it.

We can dramatically improve our life by setting goals. The importance of goal setting is espoused in most books about achievement. The simple reason for this is that goal setting truly does help to crystallise our dreams. It brings them to life by transforming them from the realms of vague, wistful fantasies and wishes to a tangible, specific and obtainable form. Setting goals helps to create a powerful vision or blueprint for the life we wish to live. When we set clear goals and maintain a focus on them we begin to attract the people and opportunities that will help to bring our dreams to fruition.

Goals need to be written as short, positive, present tense affirmations and be pitched at a realistic level. We may have to stretch to meet them, but ultimately they need to be achievable. Each success paves the way for the next success. The questions on page 248 will help you with the goal-setting process. For effective goal setting we need to ensure the following four factors are included:

Inspiration: Our goals need to propel us in the direction of the things we love and desire the most. If our goals are in keeping with our overall life purpose they will reflect our deeply held values and principles. Life-enhancing goals become self-sustaining because of the passion, pleasure and energy they bring.

Self-awareness: Self-reflection is a vital part of the goal setting process. Without it we are likely to over- or underestimate our capabilities or get out of step with our deepest needs and desires. When we set goals we need to be honest with ourselves about where we are at the outset, what changes and growth we will be required to make, what sacrifices we can foresee and whether we are prepared to make them. Open-ended goals usually fail to eventuate, so we also need to decide on a realistic time frame and commit to it. That way we can measure our progress. It's important to review our goals from time to time and modify them if they are not working.

Balance: All aspects of our life are important so we need to set goals that cover our emotional, intellectual, physical, social, financial, recreational and spiritual needs. Obviously if we are working on a big project there will be times when most of our energy is channelled in that direction, but our efforts won't be sustainable long-term if we continue to neglect ourselves and our relationships. If we try to tackle too many big goals simultaneously we are likely to fail to do justice to them and exhaust ourselves in the process, so we need to prioritise goals and pace ourselves carefully.

Small steps: Without a doubt, small steps lead to big achievements, in fact that is the only means by which important goals are achieved. Dreams are realised gradually task by task. To prevent ourselves from becoming overwhelmed on the journey we need to break our goals down into realistic small steps and focus on achieving each one within a set time frame. That way it's easy to make steady progress and to bring ourselves back on track if we are beginning to drift. The more small goals we set ourselves, the more successes we will celebrate and the more enthusiasm and confidence we will generate.

Having created our goals we need to embrace them wholeheartedly. By developing the habit of frequently reflecting on our goals they become part of our day-to-day reality and we can rekindle our passion when our interest is beginning to wane. If we are prepared to invest our time into consciously visualising a successful outcome we will be well rewarded. The clearer our vision, the sooner and more precisely we are likely to bring our dreams into reality, as the following experiences shared by Leilani Joyce and Sally Synnott demonstrate.

Leilani Joyce

' . . . you create your own destiny and opportunities.'

Winner of the 1999 and 2000 British Open Squash Tournaments, Leilani is a dynamic and positive woman. She is currently ranked the No. 1 women's squash player in the world.

Leilani was born in 1975 and grew up in Hamilton, the fourth child of a Mormon family of five. From an early age Leilani showed sporting aptitude, enjoying netball, cross-country running and swimming, but squash was to become her true love. Under her father's guidance and coaching, Leilani gradually developed her talent. He encouraged her to set goals to win her age group titles, and winning the national under-13 title remains a highlight for her. After a period of teenage rebellion Leilani has gone from strength to strength, maintaining her focus on her goals and committing herself wholeheartedly to achieving them.

Leilani was awarded the Maori Sportsperson of the Year in 1999 and Maori Sportswoman of the Year for 1998, 1999 and 2000, the first person to win this award three times. Leilani's belief in the importance of living life to the full is reflected in the enthusiasm, drive and energy she applies to her sport.

I grew up in a very sporty, competitive family. But it wasn't about winning or else. You went in and you did your best. I was 10 years old when my dad started teaching me all about goal setting and we made the ultimate goal – for me to become the best squash player in the world. Of course at that time I didn't fully understand what it was all about. I did it because he was my dad, without fully comprehending what was required. Dad would set little goals that had to be achieved, what he would term 'stepping stones'. When he was coaching me he never ever let me go into a tournament until he knew I was ready for it. And at that age it was so much fun. It was great! I was winning and my dad was there and he was my best buddy.

A lot of people thought he was too hard on me. I admit that there were times when he was tough, but the thing is that we had a vision. We had something we wanted to achieve, and there's no way that you can achieve it if you're not disciplined. So it's difficult to look back now and point the finger at him. There were times when I didn't perform properly and he'd set me right. But it must have been hard for him too, to push me when I had to be pushed. And when you've got a goal like that, sometimes that's what you might need, an extra push. That's the whole reason why I am where I am now. Because you don't become a champion by beating round the bush.

It's really quite funny because people say little kids grow up with imaginary friends. Well I didn't have an imaginary friend, I just used to talk to myself and tell myself what I was going to do. When I walked home from school I'd be saying to myself, 'When I become a really rich squash player I'm going to do this, and I'm going to do that.' It's funny because I'm 25 now and I'm doing everything I said I was going to do when I was 10 years old. That's what today I'd call visualisation. I could see it all back then. The thing about visualisation is it's like a film. You can see it happening and you feel all the emotions and you can taste it. You have a real thing for it. That was how it was for me.

At 18 I moved away from home and went through a phase where squash didn't really mean a lot to me. I lost my focus. I came to a point where I was asking, 'Who exactly am I doing this for? Is it actually my goal to be a squash champion or is it my dad's goal?' It was really like finding myself I suppose. Because I was coming up against a lot of hard competition and a different sort of training and I was asking myself, 'Is it all worth it? What do I really want to do?' That was when I started going off to all-night parties with my mates and things like that. A lot of people thought I was going off the rails, but I was just out there having a lot of fun and learning heaps.

I was at a crossroads in my life. I'd decided I was going to give up squash. But it's funny the sort of people who show up at a time like that. A close family friend gave me a poem called *Get Up and Win the Race* and it's the most amazing thing anyone's ever given me. It's about a boy who races and falls and he lays there and he's thinking, 'What am I doing this for?' Then he sees his dad's face so he gets up and keeps going each time he falls. The whole moral of the story is that winning is no more than this – to get up each time you fall. It's the sort of poem that relates to absolutely everything in your life. So that poem changed me and I decided to get back into squash again.

Now I absolutely love everything about squash. I love the sport, the opportunities I've got, the feeling of being fit and leading a healthy lifestyle. I love meeting people, the travelling, the fact that I'm able to share what I do with someone else, dealing with the media and getting invited to give talks. I admit public speaking is still nerve-wracking, but I don't worry about it so much now. And I love setting a goal and achieving that goal and being part of a huge sporting family. There's so much to it. And I reckon that's why I've done well. Because I love it so much.

I want to be competitive and share my goals and make the most of it. Because when it's over I don't want to regret anything. A lot of girls on the circuit complain about it and I'm just like, 'Why don't you stop playing if you're so unhappy? Why don't you get into something that works for you, something that you love?' I've learnt the most from the girls that have been the most negative because it spurs me on to make this work for me. One of the saddest things I heard on the circuit was, 'I'm not here to make friends.' What a sad thing to say! And what do you get? You don't get any do you! The sad reality of what you think. One of my goals is to get to know everyone on the circuit because they have so much to share.

I'm fortunate because at certain times of my life when things have been down someone has always come along and helped me in some way. Something has always happened that has pulled me through. Sometimes I look back on my life and I think, 'I'm so lucky'. But really I know that luck has got nothing to do with it, because you create your own destiny and opportunities. Being on the circuit you're vulnerable to things that can make your trip a nightmare or an absolute dream come true. I'm really fortunate to say I've never had a nightmare trip – ever. Things have always worked out well for me. I put that down to my attitude. Because if you really fret that something's going to go wrong, something will go wrong. If you consciously fear, 'I'll get burgled', I believe you will get burgled. I'm not saying that you should foolishly say that things will be OK and then go do something absolutely stupid and I'm not saying to be naive. Be smart – but enjoy it. And if you think that the best will happen, the best will happen.

I grew up with the stereotype that Maori people have got the talent but they don't have the guts. When you're younger you listen to this. And if it's said often enough you start believing it. When people used to say that to me I'd get really sad. I couldn't understand it. Just because one person has done something it doesn't mean that I'm going to do it. They didn't even know me! I became absolutely determined I wasn't going to be like that. I flatly refused to ever believe it. It's not about race at all! It's about attitude. I didn't want to end up like that so I didn't. You can be whatever you want to be, you just have to believe in yourself.

So often in my life I've come across people who put you down for wanting to succeed. That's hard and I'd be lying through my teeth if I said that it wasn't. Sometimes I don't know these people but it often comes from people who were my friends, in a situation where I've never done anything wrong. It's really hurtful. And the only reason they're doing it is because I've done well, yet I try really hard not to come across as arrogant. What they don't realise is that there's such a fine line between totally destroying someone's dreams. I'm quite sensitive and I take things personally. I admit that I'm the sort of person that always has to do things right. I always want to be everyone's mate. So when someone has a go at me for no reason, it's like, 'Wow, how can they say that?'

That's why it's so important to have a support group around you –

people who really count in your life. They don't want anything out of it, just to be there as your mate, quietly standing beside you. If any of my support crew starts saying something, I know something must be wrong because they wouldn't be saying it otherwise. Winning the British Open wasn't only an achievement for myself. We all shared in it, it was our victory because we all made it happen. It was really satisfying to say to them, 'There you go. Thanks heaps!'

My relationship with my partner Matt is very important to me. When the going gets tough – and it does and there are down times – it's so nice to share it with someone. You're not carrying it all on your own. There's someone beside you who believes in your dreams and wants to be part of them as well and to celebrate the good times. It might sound bizarre but the most important thing about winning the British Open was knowing I was going to ring Matt afterwards. Because we had just worked so hard. It's really been a partnership thing.

My life isn't just about squash. Matt and I spend a lot of time walking and just appreciating flowers and things like that. Because our lifestyle is one that is just hectic. We make time to do things like water-skiing, snow-skiing and fishing to get some balance. It's not like we have time, because we don't. But mentally it's vital because otherwise you get stale. And with squash being an indoor sport you get claustrophobic and training becomes monotonous. When everything is just that one thing and you have no other outlets it's a sad state of affairs.

When you achieve the ultimate goal you've got to have everything else in there as well to keep things balanced and in perspective, otherwise when you lose what have you got to fall back on? You haven't got anything if your sport or your ambition is the only thing in your life. So when things don't go right there's nothing left to pick you up again.

My favourite place on all this earth is Matt's parents' farm. Not only is his mum the most unbelievable cook but it's really quiet and beautiful. When I get away from the hustle and bustle of the rat race I come to realise that things aren't so bad after all. That I lost a game or that people are criticising me is not so important. I get on the farm and I sit with myself and I realise 'Who the hell are they anyway? They don't mean anything to me, these people who criticise.'

I know if I have a problem the best thing I can do is be on my own, just sit under a tree and the answers will come to me. I believe we all have the answers within ourselves. It's just whether or not we want to accept them. I know when the right answer comes because I get a special feeling inside and I know what to do. It's very satisfying and very humbling as well because afterwards I think, 'Thank goodness I followed the advice that I gave myself.' It's quite neat when something happens in your life and you see the lesson in it. I believe that everything happens for a reason. There's a lesson to be learned and if it repeats itself you obviously haven't learned that lesson.

I do appreciate life because my brother Quintin committed suicide. Things change, and so do you if you want to gain something from it. There's really so many things that I wish I'd said. I wish I could have done more. I wish I could have said goodbye. And then that person's gone! And someone as close as your brother – our only brother. Something like that happens and it opens your eyes to what really does matter. It's not buying that next big house or getting that next big flash car or that next gorgeous ring or jewellery. It really is coming home to your sisters and spending time. It's always the things that don't even cost anything isn't it?

About a month or two before my brother actually passed away I had a really interesting dream. My brother and my father and my great-great-grandfather all look the same, which is quite spooky. In this dream I actually thought it was my dad in a hospital bed. The doctor said, 'You've got three minutes to tell your dad everything that's happened in your life and then he's going to die.' It was one of those dreams where you wake up crying, you're just hysterical. Anyway we had a tangi for Quintin and we were in the marae and I just happened to be sitting there by his side, just looking at him and all these thoughts were going through my head, of times gone by and the things that have happened. Then the kaumatua got up and said, 'You've got three minutes to spend with Quintin and then we'll close his coffin and take him up to get buried.' It didn't actually dawn on me at the time about my dream until I was on the way home and it was one of those times when you get goose bumps. I feel like Quintin is always there with me.

I have a neat relationship with my family. I really do. We were little rats to each other when we were growing up but since we've got older and with me being away from home, it's made me appreciate my family. They're my sisters, my blood. Through thick and thin they're always there. It's hard to describe it. It's just that warm fuzzy feeling when I see them. My sisters are really the most amazing people. I think that I can do anything when I'm around them, because I've got my sisters. They really inspire me.

I'm very interested in the alternative forms of spirituality – very, very open to it. I totally believe in self-discovery, when you find out what is good for yourself, what you believe in, when you're there with conviction and you know without a doubt because you found out for yourself. You're not doing it because someone else is telling you that it's right. I try not to be too 'goody two shoes' if you know what I mean. I just try to just be myself. But I don't go out there to intentionally hurt anyone.

One thing I've struggled with is just believing that I am actually one of the top players now. For five years I've been following behind all the top girls admiring them and thinking, 'Wow, you're such a great squash player.' Getting there myself means I'm no longer the person who wants to be at the top. I am at the top. I've had to adjust the way that I think. I'm no longer out there trying to beat someone. I'm out there setting new standards. I'm out there achieving my goals. The challenge has been believing without a doubt that I deserve to be there. How can I become Number One if I'm forever thinking, 'Do I actually deserve this?' I could have literally let it slip from my fingers if I didn't take hold of it.

The mind is such a powerful thing. I can accept my success and gain power from it or not accept it and get back into a little comfort zone. It's easy to do if you're just not ready to take on the mantle of becoming the world champion. You can go backwards a little bit. But why? Go forward. It's that classic saying – feel the fear and do it anyway. Do it! You're here, just go with it. Believe it! If I don't succeed I can gain power from having given it a go instead of running away from it. It's not easy. I constantly work on it. I constantly run into things that I fear. You fear losing and you fear winning. With winning comes new standards and the pressure of expectations.

Over about the last two years my training has gone through the roof. It's been a combination of maturity in my mind and accepting what needs to be done. It is a conviction – I know what I want to achieve and the work that is required so I don't complain about it. I accept it and do it. I don't make excuses and I take responsibility for myself. It's not anyone else's fault if I'm not winning. At the end of the day if I haven't put the money in the bank by training it's my own fault.

I believe if we want to do something, we should do it now. I've learned to make the most of the gifts I've been given and the importance of spending the time with those who mean the most. Too often we can put a lot of time into the boss or give it to other people and forget about the ones who actually mean the most in our lives. I appreciate just being here, it's so good to be alive isn't it?

Leilani's message

Know your worth. Know what you contribute and just believe in yourself. Life is only short. Gain some sort of power from somewhere. Have the courage to get out there and give it a go. Obviously every situation is different, but it's all about knowing your self-worth in everything. Get yourself into whatever makes you happy – a relationship or a job – whatever. Not something that you have to do. Whatever you want to be, you can be. There's a saying, 'What would you do if you knew you couldn't fail?' You'd do everything! I'm really inspired by people who give it a go. Sometimes they don't succeed, but just the mere fact that they gave it a go is so empowering. Believe in yourself!

Sally Synnott

' . . . if you're doing something worthwhile and you're on to a good thing and you put enough energy into it, you do attract the people and things you need.'

Sally is the founder of Pumpkin Patch, a remark-ably successful company which specialises in children's clothes. Today the company turns over more than $100 million per year, has fifteen stores in New Zealand, thirty-five in Australia and be-tween 500–600 employees. Sally had the idea of creating Pumpkin Patch as a mail-order business in 1990. Although she was only 25, she already had four years experience as a children's wear buyer for K-Mart, a job she loved.

Sally had recognised the potential for a busi-ness such as this but she had not anticipated the phenomenal response from customers when the first catalogue went out. Both she and the sys-tems were pushed into overload for quite some time. In her third year of business, when Sally found herself pregnant with her second child five months after the birth of her first, she recognised a need to make a major lifestyle change. The perfect solution came in the form of Maurice Prendergast, who became Sally's business partner in 1994. Since then Maurice has run the business and Sally continues to be involved in strategic planning and special projects.

Despite the challenging beginnings, Sally's hard work and perseverance have paid off. Her involvement with Pumpkin Patch provides her with the joy of belong-ing to an innovative team and the satisfaction of seeing her dream continue to grow. Sally lives with her husband Mark and their three boys in Clevedon, on the family farm where she grew up.

Pumpkin Patch started from an idea I had when I was on holiday in Hawaii with some American friends. I saw a mail-order catalogue and they started telling us how they get forty or fifty catalogues a month in the post. In New Zealand we're such a widespread population I thought shopping by mail order would be a good idea. I was already working in children's wear so I knew where the gaps in the market were. I thought if I could do great quality and gorgeous designs most people would stretch themselves a bit to buy the better quality. I'd already set a goal to start my own business while my husband Mark and I were on holiday, sitting in a bar watching the sun go down. I remember Mark saying, 'You'd better really want to do it because you know when you write down a goal it always happens,' and laughing at me. Sure enough within a year it had happened.

When I had my idea I was working flat out and so I didn't really have time to follow through. Then I went to a Bob Proctor seminar called 'Born Rich', meaning that everyone is born with resources they could develop and use to create a full and satisfying life. It was a really good course and I remember Bob saying, 'If you've got a goal and you want to achieve it you've got to create a vacuum for it.' He gave an example: if you really want a new wardrobe the first thing you've got to do is chuck out the old one, whether you've got the money to replace it or not, because then you'll attract the resources you need to make your goal happen. And he said, 'Likewise, if you want a new job you've got to resign from the old one. You've got no room in your life for all these new things if you don't get rid of the old first.' That whole idea appealed to me and I thought it made sense so I resigned from my job the next day.

It really was unbelievable how within a week so much had fallen into place – finances, a corner in my friend Jeff's premises, my friend Chrissy came up with the name Pumpkin Patch and Judy, who I'd been working with before, agreed to become my right-hand person. My mind was ticking over at 100 miles an hour. A supplier I knew well came in as a fifty-fifty sleeping partner. Mark and I had to mortgage the house up to the hilt to raise our fifty per cent. We'd have lost everything if it hadn't worked but Mark was totally behind me. He always said, 'It's just a house. We can get going again.'

I really believe if you're doing something worthwhile and you're on to a good thing and you put enough energy into it, you do attract the people and things you need. I had my goal and I planned and once I set my mind to it things just fell into place. There's no way I believe now that's a coincidence because it's just happened to me too many times. If you really hold the vision and don't let any negatives come into your mind it's a really strong force. At first I thought these things were such huge coincidences. I kept saying to Mark, 'You won't believe what happened today!' and he'd say, 'It's not just coincidence you know.' It's second nature to us now.

The first six months everything went relatively smoothly as we designed and booked the clothes and produced the catalogue. But we didn't know anything about mail order. According to the theories in mail-order business you should test mailing lists by mailing to just a small percentage of each list and see who responds and then mail in quantity to the lists which work. Instead I decided I was going to risk putting our whole catalogue in with the *Little Treasures* magazine and mail it to virtually their whole list without testing it at all.

We got the first order a week earlier than we expected as we didn't realise an August issue is delivered in July and from then on we didn't put the phone down all day just taking these orders. The next day we went to get the mail and it took two of us to carry the sack back. It was so heavy! We really started to panic because our computer system wasn't 100 per cent perfect and we realised that one stand alone computer wasn't going to be anywhere near enough. So we had to try and network it. Then the computer really crashed.

The orders kept coming. It was taking us all day just to open the mail and answer the phone. We weren't getting anywhere and we were pouring more and more money into the computer system. I felt devastated but Judy was on a real high. All she could see was the success and all I could see was that we were going to let people down because I'd made a ten day delivery promise and we had no way of getting the orders out. Some of the clothes weren't ready and two or three styles came in faulty. From my perspective it was just horrific. Without Judy's positive thinking I'm not sure we would have made it.

Then the exchange rate dived. It devalued by 20 per cent over-night, which meant we lost a big chunk of our margin because the catalogues were printed with all the prices in them. With that and the computer problems the profit was basically gone. Finally Mark said to me, 'Look, we're going to have to do something because we're up to the ten days and we still haven't got an order out the door.'

We ended up hiring out the whole floor of his offices and getting twenty of our friends to work all weekend phoning every single cus-tomer. We told them the truth, 'The response has been overwhelming and our systems can't cope. We're going to have to work out some-thing manually to get the orders out. We're really sorry but it could be a few weeks.' And nobody cancelled! They were just so fantastic. They thought it was exciting and we just couldn't believe how won-derful they were. After we had rung them all our problems still weren't over because then we ran out of stock of all the most popular things. My mother was wonderful. She became known as 'The Pumpkin's Mother'. Every night she'd ring people who had waited weeks and tell them that everything they'd ordered was sold out and what was still available. People were disappointed, but Mum is just so charm-ing and genuine they still understood that things had just got out of control.

It was just a nightmare of a time. I was working from six o'clock in the morning until eleven o'clock at night. I had a friend bringing dinners in for us. It was in the middle of winter and I didn't see day-light for six weeks and I didn't look in the mirror for days at a time. Mark was coming round after work and helping. One day he brought in an entry form for a small business planning award and he said to me, 'What you need to do is to enter this.' I just about bit his head off, 'What do mean? How the hell am I supposed to write a business plan? I haven't got time!' And he said, 'Well this is the one time you need to. You've just got to sit down and evaluate where you're at and plan.' I just couldn't believe he had such a crazy idea, but in actual fact he was so right. I don't think we'd be here today if we hadn't done it.

The next season was even worse. We decided to contract out to a professional company that does fulfilment for mail-order companies. They do the telemarketing, receive the orders, hold your stock and pack and courier. But they didn't gear up for it and they made an even worse job than we had. That was just devastating! When I realised it was going wrong I just couldn't see how the business could recover. I remember bawling my eyes out while I wrote a three page letter to the customers. It started with, 'We must have made every mistake in the book . . .' I explained everything and asked if they would give us a third chance, even though we didn't deserve it. We also sent everyone a Christmas card that year to say how sorry we were. That was a ten thousand dollar exercise but it was definitely the right thing to do. We got a lot of wonderful feedback, but I think some people thought we were going to go broke after reading the letter. Probably about 80 per cent of them gave us another chance, and luckily the next season went like clockwork.

During those early days there were times when I felt desperate to get away. I remember at my most desperate stage not being able to stop crying. One night Mark and I were lying in bed and I said, 'I just can't stand doing this anymore. I just have to have a life.' That was the only time Mark ever got angry about it and he just said, 'Look, let me tell you right now you can stop this business tomorrow. I don't mind if you do. I'm quite happy to start again. We'll work to pay everyone back and you can just walk away. You won't be a disappointment to me.' It was just like I'd been given this huge injection of energy. I started to think, 'I don't want to give up!' I'd been feeling extremely trapped but once I had a way out it was OK. I could keep going.

My older sister Katie, who has been my best friend all my life, managed our first shop and was the only other person to really get through to me, she made me see the successes as well as the disasters. She said, 'At least everyone loves the catalogue. How would you feel if the problem was no orders?'

I felt desperate again when I found myself pregnant five months after my son Jack was born. I knew I wasn't capable of being a full-time working mother and I didn't want to be anyway so I decided to sell the business. I really knew I needed to get some balance back in my life but I felt devastated that I was giving up my dream.

Sometimes I wonder at how much luck I've had in my life, first of all to have Chrissy join us and take over the designing and then to get a partner like Maurice. He'd somehow heard a rumour that I was going to sell and so we got together and we hit it off straightaway. We put a deal together really quickly and luckily he wouldn't let me sell out completely. So I'm involved in special projects and the strategic planning now and I've always got something pretty exciting on the horizon. Maurice is the Managing Director and he's never interfered in the marketing side of it at all but he's fixed all the areas that needed fixing, such as the systems and the finance. I still love being involved. I thought I'd get to the stage where I'd just want to be off doing something else, but Pumpkin Patch is a bit like a baby to me now.

I'm definitely passionate about the business but at times my passion has been directed elsewhere, like family. That's where it's been wonderful having Maurice because he's just quite happy for me to step aside when I need to. It's the perfect thing for me because I'm not a stayer. I'm a starter and I know that. I'm an ideas person. That's a strength but it also gives you a weakness, because if you can't maintain something well day to day it'll soon fall apart. I always know when I'm under major stress because I dive into the detail which I'm useless at. When I started out I was drawn to people who had the same strengths as me but that doesn't make for a strong team. It's been a real learning curve to acknowledge my weaknesses and employ people in those areas and really give them the responsibility.

Mark has been a huge influence in my life. He believed in me right from when I first met him when I was 18 years old. I remember I wanted to apply for a job and you had to be a minimum of 25 and have at least ten years' experience, and I was straight out of design school. He said, 'Go for it. We'll put together a CV and if you can get an interview I bet you get the job.' So we wrote this letter and I did something my father had once done. I said, 'Look, I'll work for half the salary and if you don't think I'm good at the job at the end of six months at least it will only cost you half the money.' And I got the job.

There was a similar situation later on when I saw a job in the paper with a great salary and a car and I had no experience in that area at all. I begged and begged to be given an interview and the consultant wouldn't and Mark said, 'Go up there and sit in his office until he gives you an interview.' That was a pretty scary thing to do at 21 but I flew up from Wellington to Auckland dressed in a beautiful suit I had designed and made myself. I remember waiting outside his office and the receptionist was trying to make me go away. Finally after he'd been in one of these long interviews for about an hour and a half he came out and I stood up and said, 'Hi, I'm Sally. I've been trying to get an appointment with you,' and he just burst out laughing and said, 'Well, I guess that deserves five minutes.'

Three and a half hours later I'd done all the tests and had an interview scheduled for the morning. Mark said to me, 'Look you've got to sell them on the spot, because if you walk away from that interview they're going to start thinking logically, "Hang on a minute we've got all these applicants and they've got the experience and she hasn't. We shouldn't really take a risk." So don't walk out of there without the job.'

In the interview I felt like I was going along fine and then they said, 'We'll call you,' and I said, 'Look I really want this job but I'm going to another interview in a moment. It's my final interview for that job and if I leave here not knowing if I've got this job I'm going to completely convince myself that I want that job and put my heart and soul into getting it, and if I get the job I'm going to accept it.' They couldn't believe what they were hearing and they said, 'Just a minute we need to talk to each other,' and so I left the room thinking, 'I don't believe I'm doing something so cheeky. I'm going to get kicked out of here.'

Anyway, they called me back in and they were laughing and they said, 'We think you deserve a job.' As I left the building I tried to appear so cool and calm. My brother was waiting for me outside and as soon as I saw him I ran over screaming and threw my arms around his neck. Little did I know they had come to the cafeteria at the front of the building and saw the whole thing and they apparently laughed their heads off.

So I became the children's wear buyer for K-Mart. The first time I went to buy something I was terrified. I was so determined that I was going to get a good price and when I left, the salesman's boss rang my marketing manager and said, 'We have just done this deal with your buyer and we're going to lose money on it.' My boss said, 'Hard luck, sort it out with Sally.' I ended up giving them more money for it, much to their surprise. My father had always brought me up to believe that both sides have to win. You've got to leave something in it for the next guy and always be fair and make sure that everyone comes out of a deal well. At least I stopped worrying about not being able to negotiate after that.

Thanks to Mark, constant planning has been really important to me. It sounds controlled but in actual fact the more planning I do, the more I live in the moment. Mark and I always have a good goal setting session once a year but we usually sit down midyear and see if we're on top. When we set goals we usually go somewhere we can relax. Our basic procedure is to set the clock and spend two minutes writing down everything we ever want to achieve in our lives, just brainstorming anything that comes into our mind without stopping to think about it. We're going for quantity at that stage, not quality. Then we spend another two minutes just looking over what we've written. Then we do the same thing for five year's time and also as if we've only got six months to live.

Usually by the time you've done your three lists it's fairly clear what your goals are going to be for the next year, but often something unexpected will come out and when you stop and analysis it you realise it's something you'd really like to do. In each list you've got to prioritise your top four or five goals because you just can't do everything. You can't write a book, run a business, have six kids and be an Olympic athlete. They might all be dreams but something has to fall out, so you have to choose. A lot of people think it's hilarious that we plan our life, but we find it doesn't take the spontaneity out of our life. It keeps us focused and it's a fun thing to do.

I've done a lot of courses over the years. I think they can be incredibly valuable as long as you go with an open mind and just look for one or two good ideas. About four years ago I went to one by Stephen Covey, *First Things First*. His theory is you need to plan for all parts of your life. You sit down at the beginning of each week and plan your week. You block in time with your family and friends, time for your fitness and time for your own reflecting. Those are really the important things you can't do without. Then you plan your work around that. That's been hugely valuable for me.

I have a simple time management and planning system Mark designed years ago that's had a huge impact on the way I've worked. It's a really basic idea of always writing things in a book. I have a red book which I use for everything – writing names, phone numbers, thoughts and letters. I staple cards or ideas into it. If I'm designing something I'll draw in it. I just use it constantly. I have a planner sheet that has my week's appointments down one side. Now that I've done *First Things First* I block in my personal things first, so I don't get to the end of the week and feel completely wrenched because I haven't had any time for myself or I haven't done any exercise. I paste the planner sheet in at the beginning of the week on the next blank page. It might take me twenty pages of notes before the next week or two but I'm not confined by a certain amount of space to write in, as you are with a diary. No matter how busy I am, I spend the first fifteen minutes of the day evaluating what I've got to get done and re-prioritising. I've found that just frees my mind so much because anything I write down I don't have to remember.

Of course my goals have changed a lot over the years. The stage I'm at, my goals are centred around balance and my family and my friends and I get a lot of pleasure out of the little things now. Each night I spend ten or fifteen minutes in bed talking with my two older boys. If you actually really slow down and listen to them, it's amazing what they will tell you. Their little minds are gorgeous! I love just spending time with Mark at night sitting in front of the fire having a chat. I go running a lot with a really good friend and we talk and we share everything. I can't really describe how much living on our farm with our extended family means to me. Being part of the land and being able to get out in the bush or the hills. I've grown up with that and it's a part of me.

Giving is probably one of the most enjoyable things you can do and I've certainly learnt the more you give the more you receive. At the moment Mark and I are setting up a charitable trust. The dream behind it is to give money to young New Zealanders who aren't going to be able to achieve by their own means and see if I can motivate and also financially get them through their education. I've been incredibly lucky myself and I get a huge kick out of seeing other people succeed.

Sally's message

You're born with as much ability as the next guy to achieve your dreams. You've got, or can get, what it takes so just believe in that 1000 per cent. Concentrate on your strengths and understand what your weaknesses are and recognise that the balances to those weaknesses are in other people, so involve them too.

The importance of positive thinking, having a vision and goal setting is bandied around so much, but it's just so true that setting goals and believing in them is powerful. I believe there's a positive force or energy out there we can all tap into. When you've got a clear goal you attract the resources. There has to be something that's a force out there and some way that we are all connected, because you can't have those millions of so-called coincidences without it.

Realise that nothing can be done without a team so don't be selfish. Help make other people's lives full and satisfying by really believing in them, involving them, and giving responsibility and appreciation. Two quotes I've heard that I love are 'catch people doing things right, not wrong' and 'seek first to understand, then to be understood'.

Sally Synott

When you go for your dream you've got to be sure that it's what you really want, because it's really going to throw your life out of balance for a time. In my case it took a long time before I could say it was worthwhile. Now I definitely think it was worthwhile. It gives me so much pleasure.

So set your goals and keep evaluating your plan and go to a course to be refreshed by somebody's new ideas at least on a yearly basis if you can. Plan when you're in your most desperate stage and you really don't think you've got the time and just believe in it 1000 per cent and it will happen.

COMMITTING
TO ACTION

Every day thousands of people bury good ideas because they are afraid to act on them. And afterwards the ghosts of those ideas come back to haunt them.

The Magic of Thinking Big, David J. Schwartz

The dreams that call us to live life out loud begin as a wish, desire, hope or bright idea. It takes action to bring them to fruition. The period between having the idea and bringing it into a tangible form can be especially challenging. This is where dreams become abandoned or lost. Sometimes we need time to grow into our dreams when they take us into new territory, outside our limits of knowledge and confidence. People who have become highly successful in their chosen fields have done so because they have continued to stretch themselves by gaining new knowledge and skills to meet the challenges new pursuits present. We too can find the courage to do this.

Often our dreams require an incubation period where we work away quietly strengthening and solidifying them, collecting the information necessary to allow us to make an informed decision about whether to proceed. We research the viability of our idea by reading or speaking to relevant people, working out costs and brainstorming how to overcome possible difficulties. We rehearse it in our mind and debate the pros and cons to gain clarity. This is an important part of the journey but during this time it's vital to maintain our optimism and ensure we don't talk ourselves out of ideas which have the potential to succeed.

We need to choose wisely who we share our embryonic dreams with, as they can be fragile and easily destroyed by others' criticism. Sharing prematurely can deplete our energy and excitement, especially if we receive a lukewarm or negative response. While some people may raise our enthusiasm and provide us with valuable feedback, we are usually best to hug our dream to ourselves if we are worried about withstanding possible negativity. When we have developed a clear vision of our dream and have created a plan of action by breaking it down into manageable steps, we are better prepared to face the doubters.

As we reflect on our dreams it's important to be realistic about what pursuing that particular course of action will require of us. We set ourselves up for failure by underestimating the challenges we may face. Very few dreams can be achieved without overcoming particular hurdles, especially at the outset. These hurdles may include lack of time, finance, support, knowledge, childcare, skills or confidence. At first glance these issues can seem daunting but usually if we focus on them one at a time and approach each one as a problem-solving exercise we will find creative ways around them.

Sometimes when we have a big dream and we can't see where the resources will come from to enable us to achieve it, it may be necessary to leave something to chance. While it's important to be practical and pitch our dreams at a realistic level, it's also important to allow enough space for surprises to occur. At the outset we are not able to see all the many events that may conspire in our favour to bring our dreams into reality. Potential difficulties have a way of being overcome when we move confidently towards our goals.

The real power to achieve our heart's desire comes when we are prepared to commit to it. A dream without a commitment is simply a wish. It's very powerful to decide to do whatever it takes to make it happen. With commitment comes the increased determination, energy and focus vital to success.

Having made the decision to go for it, it's sometimes difficult to know where to begin, but usually it doesn't matter where we start — just that we do! Inevitably we will learn as we go, make mistakes and have occasional failures. There are likely to be times when we feel out of our depth, scared and overwhelmed. That is all part of the process.

When we commit to our dream with all our heart, have a positive attitude and actively work towards it, something very powerful often starts to happen. Things begin to fall into place in very unexpected ways. Some would call this divine intervention, others would say it is serendipity, synchronicity, coincidence or luck. Whatever force we understand this to be, time after time people experience it. Their situation changes in surprising ways to create exactly the right circumstance to propel them towards their dream. They meet the right person, find the right book, are offered the right opportunity or encounter a new piece of information that throws a whole new light on things. Many of us have had this experience and have learned to trust and delight in it.

When we are working towards our goals it is important to keep the momentum going. We are not always going to be highly productive. Sometimes we will have an off day and need to pull back and take care of ourselves, but even then it is often possible to take some very small steps towards our goal. If we allow ourselves to grind to a complete standstill and let our dream go cold, it can be difficult to get moving again. If our excitement begins to wane we need to refocus and recommit. By spending some time visualising the accomplished dream, reminding ourselves about how it will feel to achieve it and why we want it, we can regenerate our passion and enthusiasm. Over time we are likely to be amazed at the ground we cover if we just keep going. Mountains are climbed one step at a time.

Vicki Buck and Caron Taurima are two women who have experienced the satisfaction of bringing big dreams to fruition. Their stories demonstrate how with optimism, creativity and perseverance bright ideas can be transformed into great achievements.

Vicki Buck

'I think you can achieve way more if you're actually enjoying it . . .'

Vicki began her twenty-three year career in local body politics in 1974, when at the age of 19 she was elected to the Christchurch City Council. She was the popular mayor of Christchurch from 1989 until 1998. Known for her positive 'can do' approach, vision and enthusiasm, Vicki brought enormous changes to Christchurch during her nine years as mayor.

Although she loved Christchurch she had found it a boring city to grow up in and was passionate about making it a more exciting place, as well as tackling the social issues dear to her heart. Most people would agree she succeeded. During her time as mayor Vicki was the driving force behind the city's lively festivals and outdoor entertainment and led the city in social projects such as the strategy for children, major employment programmes and a city enhancement project which includes a new convention centre, sports and entertainment centre, art gallery and the revitalisation of the city. She was also committed to a 'hands on' approach to local body politics, addressing social issues such as unemployment, poverty and housing in a forthright way.

Vicki has her own company and currently works as a development manager for Christchurch Polytechnic, and is a director and part owner of the Christchurch School of English. She also sits on the new Science and Innovation Council, on the boards of Netball New Zealand and Jade Stadium and is a member of Te Papa's National Services Advisory Committee.

I think we undervalue the amazing potential we all have in terms of what we can do. I like the 'just do it' sort of approach. I don't like the word 'should'. I believe there doesn't necessarily need to be a big plan – especially a strategic plan – in fact I think they're counterproductive. You can just go and make it happen. I think there is a huge potential within each of us that we don't use. Some people have this idea that you have to work hard, and I suppose that's true in some regards, but I think there are often ways of doing things that just require thinking differently or creatively.

I love ideas. They get me into trouble all the time because I tend to process information by talking it through with other people. Often if I'm with people I'll get another ten or twelve ideas. I was sitting having coffee with a group of friends about two years ago and we were thinking about young kids and their inventiveness and we decided we should create a thing called Young Invention and put it on in the Convention Centre and invite all the schools. It was great fun talking about it but then we had to do it! There are way too many ideas to actually do them all and ideas are way too easy. It can be troublesome!

I have a belief that I can do things and so can everybody else. I probably have a slight disregard or disrespect for traditional rules and for beliefs that are limiting. I just don't accept limiting beliefs such as 'you can't possibly be mayor in Christchurch because you come from the wrong side of the tracks or because you're female or because you're not well off'. I think they're just nonsense! They cannot possibly be true. They're just perceptions that people have created for themselves.

When I announced I was standing for mayor I decided to stand as an independent, which was not the done thing. I was also pregnant with my first child. This story came out all over the front page of the newspaper that you can't be mayor and a mother. Then all these older women, maybe in their late sixties and seventies, started ringing me and saying, 'Just don't believe these things. We've had to be bound by these rules all our lives and we just think they're so bloody stupid!' And they just rang and rang. They were just stunning! It was one of the best weekends I've ever had. They were people I didn't know, but they were so passionate about it.

When I was standing for mayor I wasn't well known. There were no funds from parties for campaigning because it was an independent campaign so we had to do things that were different to grab attention. I actually think doing something differently can be not only satisfying but really a smart thing to do. Just because it's always been done a certain way in the past I don't think that is the prescription for how it has to be done in the future. So in the past people had campaigned in a certain way. Well that would have been great if we had $50,000 but we didn't, so we rigged the car up with the loudspeaker with a really cool campaign song so everyone noticed. My dad made a desk turned upside down with billboards around it and stuck it on the car. We had an office right in the middle of town so people could come and help.

We weren't allowed to go into malls to give out political leaflets so we got daffodils and just put a little label with my name on them – because that wasn't political material – and gave them to people. It was amazing because you give someone a flower and first of all they're really pleased and then what do you do with a flower? Especially after an hour because it's all wilted and you can't chuck it out. But they take it anyway. So every day I'd get sent out with this boot load of daffodils to try and get myself into a mall or stand on the street corner.

I think having the capacity to do things differently and have a lot of fun along the way is really, really important. I believe you can actually create things that you do enjoy so why would you do things that you don't enjoy? Being aware that there are always opportunities and it's just a matter of plugging yourself into them is probably something I've developed with age. When I left university and I was first looking for a job I didn't have that sense that I could just go and create my own business. I felt like I needed to earn some money. I was unemployed for six or seven months, then driving taxis and trucks with a masters degree. That's when I became very interested in the issue of unemployment because I knew what it did to me. It was a very shitty thing to go through and very destroying of dreams and self-esteem.

It certainly made me acutely aware that unemployment was a major issue. I think it's a criminal waste of human potential, because it traps individuals. It doesn't allow them to realise their capabilities. It just squashes them. I hate it. It's revolting! So when I was on the council unemployment was a key issue for me.

My childhood was fairly unremarkable. There were five kids in the family. I'm right in the middle. It felt safe and secure even though there was never any money. Mum and Dad were usually in their own business, although Mum was always home after school so I felt as if she was there for me. They did a whole range of things like running dairies and motels. Then Dad went into gold mining – all sorts of weird things. They were both from very poor, large families of nine or ten, way down south. Dad's dad had left when he was quite young so Dad went out to work when he was about seven, selling newspapers to try to supplement the family income. He left school after the end of primary school to go working. Mum had left school after primary school to go working too, despite the fact that she desperately wanted to go on. So Mum's big thing was the importance of education. Reading was highly valued and we'd always go down to the library on a Wednesday night to get out as many books as we were allowed. There was a lot of discussion of political issues and you had to be reasonably assertive to get your point across at the dinner table.

I first got involved in politics at 16 when I went to university. I actually found my first year at university quite boring in terms of the subjects so I got involved in the Labour Party and all sorts of groups. So my education was mainly outside of the lecture theatres.

I was 19 when I was first elected to the council. The council was largely men who were much older than me. It was really annoying for them when I was able to speak and when I wanted to change things that was even more annoying. So they did the 'we'll try to ignore her' technique. That was seriously hard! It's actually very rude when you go into the council and people just completely ignore you. The most annoying thing for them was I tended to get a lot more publicity than them because I was young and female and at varsity and interested in changing things. Despite all that I really did enjoy my work with the council and things did improve. Some of them even gave me donations later on when I stood for mayor. That was really amazing!

While I was on the Local Government Commission I actually applied to Canterbury University to do a PhD and they said no I couldn't because I was in 'meaningful employment'. So I argued that being on the Local Government Commission was not meaningful employment at all. They didn't seem to agree with that and I still wasn't allowed, so I decided to read all the books I could find on how our brain worked instead. I learned how we have this amazing mechanism and we know very little about the way it works and we don't teach thinking as a skill. The make-up of each person's brain is completely different, so what they'll take in and what they'll think about will be different from anybody else. So their construct of the world is absolutely unique. That's like, far out! Wow! Because each of us has an absolutely unique view of the world I feel we've got some sort of obligation to use our brain because never in the history of humanity will it be there again. I discovered a lot about how we can put thoughts and belief structures into our brain and how we can actually choose the thoughts that get in there. That changed my view of what we're capable of. It's a subject I just love. I just love the process of thinking and teaching creative thinking. It's really, really interesting.

The master in that field is Edward de Bono. I think his book *The Mechanism of Mind,* which is the very early one he wrote, is as good as any in terms of describing how the brain organises information. I've met him three or four times when we got him out here to speak to a whole pile of school kids. We're actually in the process of setting up the de Bono Creative Thinking Foundation for New Zealand.

For me motivation comes from within and if somebody tells me to do something that's a very bad reason for doing it. It just wouldn't have enough excitement about it. Of course I'd do it if it was part of the job I was being paid for, but I'd just do it. I wouldn't be thinking of a better way to do it or anything like that.

I've now become quite passionate about changing or providing choice within the primary education system and having been exposed to it I think there are major weaknesses within it. The fear I have is that it takes really creative, wonderfully imaginative little kids and seeks to provide conformity and obedience and discipline. I find that scary in a time when those kids are probably going to have to create their own jobs.

At the moment I chair a trust which is about to start a new state primary school. It's just got approval from the Minister, which is just awesome. It's something I believe passionately in. We've spent a lot of hours each week for nearly two years just putting this together. It's completely unpaid obviously, but it's something I'm really excited about. There is just so much that needs to be done. I guess that's part of why I got into politics. I think the best reason to get into politics is because you're really passionate about things and you want to change something, because it's a really good means of doing that. Politics is something I've always loved and I guess it's sort of a mild addiction that you probably never really recover from.

I'd describe myself as optimistic and also probably stubborn in some ways, in that I don't believe there are things that can't be done. If somebody says something like, 'There are only two ways you can do this', I am immediately switching off from what they're saying and I'm finding ways three, four and five. I hate the idea that there are limitations or boundaries or constrictions on what you can do. I also see the funny side of things and that can get me into trouble.

I actually think laughing is really important. It's one of those things that keep us fit and healthy. It gives some balance in things. I think you can achieve way more if you're actually enjoying it and having a good time along the way because then it doesn't feel like work. I get bored quite easily, so in meetings I have to find some humour to keep myself sitting still. I think meetings need to be entertaining and funny. There is so much about life that is seriously funny. Laughing gets you through a lot of situations that could otherwise be very stressful and it has a very good effect on your brain physiology as well. I think if you're generally having a good time then you tend to be optimistic about things so they go much easier, so that's self-sustaining in a way.

For some people life is a serious matter and they believe you should not be having fun while you're doing it. I don't think life is a serious matter and I can see how some people regard that as annoying. The thing that intrigues me about people's attitudes is that if you're really negative and serious and believe 'this is hard' then in a lot of people's minds that's realistic. So being optimistic about things, 'Yeah sure we can do that, and we can probably cut a bit of time off if we did it this way, or we could do it a completely different way, or there's probably twelve different ways we could do it. Which way do you feel like doing it today?' is not seen as realistic. To be 'realistic' you have to be negative about things, which I think is odd.

It's difficult for me to distinguish work from play because a big chunk of work feels like play. I can achieve a lot that way. I don't necessarily have very good boundaries between work and play and family and other things. Most days I can just zoom through stuff and none of it's an effort. I don't expect things to feel difficult so if they do there's usually a reason for it. I know it's really important to listen to my body. It's sort of an intuitive thing. If something doesn't feel right I don't ignore that. That signal's too precious. I'd tend to stop and pay some attention to myself, rather than try to rationalise it out. I expect my body to work perfectly all the time but because I abuse it with coffee and diet coke and junk food and glasses of wine then I should nurture it. If it's telling me it's tired or stressed in some way I should actually pay attention to that. My gym routine would be called 'Twenty Minutes is Heaps', because I never do the programme. I only do what I feel like at the time.

I think living in New Zealand is very lucky in terms of life's chances. It's such an incredible lottery where we're born. Here we can do a children's programme and make sure the kids have a really great time but that doesn't mean the kids in Mozambique are not going to die of malaria. And once you've seen them it's something that you carry with you. It's not fair and it's not just and it's not acceptable. I don't think we can just glibly say that everything is fine and rosy because we're having a good time here. I don't feel that sort of separation. I think there are some things that are seriously hard. I don't think we can just walk away and pretend it's OK, because everything is not OK in the world. That's part of the reason why I'll always believe in having safety nets for people.

I have huge respect for people who have done things they've really believed in, quite often in a major personal crisis. It was an incredible joy of being the mayor that I actually got to meet a lot of inspiring people who do a huge amount every day, often with limited physical capacity. Like they'll be in a wheelchair or they'll be blind and they just do phenomenal things. They make you feel wow! You feel lazy by the time you finish talking to them. I think those people can be so inspirational to us all.

Vicki's message

I think the most important thing about achieving dreams is having that clear dream in the first place. Because then you can probably actually see yourself doing it. You can probably almost taste it and know how it will feel when you're there. And I think that's a really important driving force, probably even more so for women, because often for women it seems that it's not about material rewards, it's about something that's more untouchable.

So if you've got a clear dream I'd say you're more than halfway there. If there are barriers then just go round them. Those barriers never occupy the entire span of human endeavour. There's always a way round or over or under or through. Especially if you know that's what you want to do. If you're really charged up then no barrier can stand in the way of that. You can do anything. Because of the incredible brain power each one of us has got, there aren't boundaries and there aren't limitations. So if you've got a clear dream, however long the road is, you're already there.

Caron Taurima

'There's so many opportunities out there – so much untapped.'

Caron is the founder and current CEO of Carich Training Centre, a private multimedia and technology training academy working with people from unemployed to corporate level. The company employs up to 100 staff and has up to 700 people attending courses on any one day. Located in five centres, Carich has produced and funded a successful Maori language CD-ROM which has been distributed free of charge to schools throughout the country. They have also produced CD-ROMs on traffic safety, driving and alcohol.

Caron's business began in 1988 with a bright idea. Caron was 21, had just moved to Christchurch and was unemployed. Her main skill was in computers so she decided to set up a computer training programme. Unable to raise the money to start up in business from the bank, Caron convinced her father to mortgage 90 per cent of his house to raise the $65,000 needed. Determined to pay back this loan, she threw herself into her work using the combination of vision, commitment and hard work that has created her success.

Caron's achievement in business has been recognised by three awards. In 1995 she received the Maori Women's Development award for the best small business and in 1996 she was awarded the NZIM Young Executive of the Year for the southern region. In 1999 Caron was the winner of the Maori Women's Business Award for Overall Excellence in Business. Caron is married to Richard Taurima and they have four children.

When I decided to go into business I'd just turned 21 and I couldn't get a job. It was exciting and it was scary. But you take more risks when you're younger. I believed I could do it, so I just went from there. Before that I hadn't really known what I wanted to do. I'd had about five or six jobs and I didn't stay at any for longer than a year. I'd helped a guy to set up a computer training centre in Wellington, then we moved to Christchurch and I contacted him and asked him if he'd set one up in Christchurch and let me manage it. When he said no I was very disappointed. I had all these wonderful ideas! But then once I got over that I thought, 'Well, why don't I do it myself?'

I just wanted to have a job and I couldn't get any money together so I convinced Dad to mortgage his house and I went from there. All I really had was myself, some good ideas and some basic computer skills. That was what I enjoyed and I didn't really know much else.

When I first started the business it was just, 'Heads down, let's work to get this going.' I was driven by responsibility of making sure my dad didn't lose his house and I was determined to succeed. We set up one small training room with a computer suite and we advertised in the paper to do a training course. Six people applied and I taught them for twelve weeks and everyone got a job out of that. I did it all. I was the receptionist, the cleaner, the tutor – everything.

I applied for funding to run more courses and we got another and another course so I started hiring people and just grew from there. Once we got up to about six courses we started looking at what else could we do with our resources. Where else could we go? Over the years we've grown a lot. In the last three years we've expanded to five sites and we've gone into fee paying now. Students apply for student loans and they'll come out now with international qualifications as computer technicians or they'll learn how to do computer graphics or animation or things like that. So it's really exciting.

In the beginning I'd never have envisaged getting so big. I've wanted to do lots of things to expand over the years but we had to expand when we had enough money and there's never been enough to do everything so it's been a matter of making choices. There are always risks but I believe that if we've got a quality product, we're doing what we should be doing, we're doing it well and we're looking after our staff, which is really our best asset, we can't go wrong. We'll have people coming to us. It's when you're not delivering to people's expectations that you have problems.

I've made mistakes but that's all part of it. As long as we're learning from them and making things right so they don't happen again I don't mind. It's when that mistake happens again that there's something wrong. On any one day about 700 students come through the centres. We can't keep everybody happy 100 per cent of the time, but as long as we're doing our best to try keep the majority happy and making sure we've got things in place to look after everybody we're on the right track.

Even though I'm the CEO and Chairperson of the Board and I'm now looking at the company from a strategic point of view, I still dive in and do stuff because I still want to be involved. I've found just walking around and sitting in the classrooms will tell me how well we're actually delivering products and services. Once a month I'll go to each of the centres and have a chat with the students. It's not about, 'What are we doing wrong?' It's a 'How's it going?' just to get a feel of what's actually happening. I've got a little bit of a knack now. I know just by walking past a classroom whether or not the tutor's doing a good job. It's just something that you pick up as you go. Every one of those tutors standing in front of the classroom is actually representing me and I take it very personally if people don't take a pride in their work.

One of the things I've learnt is that you need to get the right people into the right jobs. I haven't got the skill base now to look after a larger company so I'm better to get other people in to do it or give people opportunities to learn. I don't need to know everything. I just concentrate on what I'm good at. Now when we're hiring staff we can pay more to get better people and that makes a big difference.

When I first started out there were hardly any support services for people in business so I looked around at other business people I knew to see how they tackled things. I'd meet people and I'd think, 'I really like what they do', and I'd just take out the bit that meant something to me and then either implement it or try and mould myself to that way. I was quite stubborn and I worked out a lot of things for myself, but now I don't have a problem getting on the phone and asking people for help. Now if I've come across a particular issue I know which person will be able to help me. I'm on several different boards and this gives me a lot of personal development. I've just learned so much from other people who've got a lot of experience behind them looking after large organisations. I've realised people are usually very happy to help. I think sometimes they're even pleased that they have been called. It's the same with me. People call me and I don't have a problem helping them or telling them where I think they should go for help.

My creativity is almost like a street-smart type of creativity. I'm very good at ideas. People will say, 'You can't do this', but I'll be able to figure out how to get from here to there. I've become very good at snooping around and finding someone who knows someone to tell me where to go to get what I need. And I know I can talk people into making it happen. So that's where my creativity is. And I'm probably good at negotiating – good at selling the person the benefits. It's being able to think of different ways of presenting what you do. It may not always work. I may get a 'no' but the next time I come back I just try to present it a different way.

As a child my parents did have a very good influence on me. I was instilled with this belief that I could do anything. Whenever I had a weird idea about what I was going to do they never, ever said, 'Oh you can't do that'. They always said, 'Well, how are you going to do that?' or 'That's a great idea.' I'd hear them talking to other people about us and saying how good we were at things – whether we were or not.

When I was little we weren't very well off as a family, but my dad and my mum worked in self-employment opportunities. If we wanted money we used to pick the fruit from the plum trees in the back yard and we were allowed to keep the money from what we sold. I remember making ginger beer in Dad's old beer bottles and selling it and making these round sheepskin things with little arms. I think they were called gonks at the time. We made them in class and I thought, 'I could sell these', and all my aunties felt sorry for me and bought them for 50c. It was my choice to go away to boarding school, so in the holidays I waitressed to pay for the airfares and the clothes I needed because my dad couldn't afford to pay for those things. Really it came down to the fact that I had to work for what I wanted.

I've learnt in business as I've gone along. I started an MBA by correspondence but because I was very busy I found that I didn't have enough time to complete it. I did do a few papers and I implemented what I learned into my business. I've been to speak at quite a few university lectures and polytechs and organisational things. At the end of the speeches the lecturers usually say, 'Well when Caron was speaking about this, that's this theory and when she was talking about this happening, that's that model.' So while I don't actually know the technical terms for what I'm doing the principles are still the same. I suppose it's really theory in practice.

I work on a thing called common-sense management – if it doesn't make common sense I don't do it. Intuition is a big part of that and I think it's that street awareness as well. The two are interconnected. Everything that I've learnt comes into play. I believe intuition is built on experience, so the more experience you've got, the better your intuition and gut instinct is.

I think because I'm the eternal optimist I don't actually see the tough times. I don't stress a lot, there's no point in getting angry because yelling and jumping up and down isn't going to solve the problem. You're better to channel that energy into figuring out what you can do to make it right. If things are going really wrong I think, 'In three months time I'll look back on this and learn from it.' Or if staff leave I see this as a good thing as well as bad. The good thing is that it's great for the person. They can move on and expand their horizons. But as well as that it provides an opportunity for fresh blood to come into the company and new ideas and new initiatives and people with better experience to come in.

I like reading business books. I remember reading *Rich Dad Poor Dad* about six years ago and finding Robert Kiyosaki's philosophies very good. I also like reading about other organisations and how they started up – what they did and how they did it. I'll read a book from cover to cover over a day or so and I'll just pick little bits and pieces out that I agree with or that will inform me. I especially like reading about people who were just normal everyday people who come up with a fabulous product and went from whoa to go and achieved what they set out to do. That's just incredible and I really admire those people.

Having a supportive partner is so important in business. I taught a course called *Be Your Own Boss* for women and I noticed that a lot of the women came from homes where their partners didn't support them. They were always put down. When I'd say positive things to them their comments would be, 'Oh, I couldn't do that', or 'I'm not good enough to do that.' It was that continual negativity coming through but because it was a twelve-week course the women started getting motivated and feeling good. If they had someone at home saying, 'This is great. What can I do to help?' they'd just blossom, but this wasn't the case for many of them. I'd notice they'd have a really good week and then they'd come back deflated after the weekend. But they weren't quite back in the rut and they'd slowly build up. At the graduation they'd often be crying saying, 'Thank you so much for what you've done.' They'd actually gained confidence in themselves more than anything.

Goal setting is important for me. I believe that goals are powerful, especially when they're written down. When I was 15 I wrote a list of goals in my journal. I wanted to own a million dollar business and to travel the world. That was in 1982. That was just something that I did at that time but it's amazing what's come out of it. I believe you need to condition yourself to success. When I can visualise what I want the motivation is there to make it happen.

My business goals tend to take over my personal goals and trying to find a balance can be quite hard going. Once a year I revise my personal goals. I used to carry them around in my wallet on a little laminated card but I haven't done that for a while now. Nowadays just continuing to make this work is enough.

I believe that if you do things that are right and are a good person you will be blessed. I believe that for anybody. It doesn't matter what religion you are. Same as if you rip people off and you're dishonest, your time will come. When I'm making decisions I'll always make sure they are within the bounds of what my beliefs are. I won't compromise or do something dishonest. I'd rather be upfront, have everything out on the table then you know exactly where you are and there's no hidden surprises. There have been lots of opportunities to be involved in things that aren't right but I just won't do it. It's just not worth it!

Caron's message

Don't let other people influence what you actually want to do. Do something that you enjoy, and enjoy it as you go. Of course it's not always going to be fun, but it can be more satisfying working for yourself than for somebody else. And if you've got a really good product that people want the money will come. While money is important it's not the most important thing. It's not that I do what I do for the money. I do it because I love it. I believe if you're doing something you enjoy and you're doing it well — it will all come together. The money's a given.

There's room in the world for lots more people in business. There's so many opportunities out there — so much untapped. Anybody can do it if they're determined enough. I just had UE, no great background in terms of wealth or anything like that. Don't be afraid to ask people for help; you get some really great contacts. Just put your mind to it and do it.

OVERCOMING DOUBTS AND FEARS

All you have to do to diminish your fear is to develop more trust in your ability to handle whatever comes your way!

Feel the Fear and Do It Anyway, Susan Jeffers

Self-doubt and fear are the inner obstacles that stand between people and their dreams. If we are to live life fully we need to move out of our comfort zone and to stretch our skills and confidence by tackling new things. As we do we are likely to come up against our fears. We may be afraid of being seen as inadequate or proved incompetent, of being humiliated or ridiculed, of failure, change and even success. It's quite natural to feel apprehensive when we do something new, but it's vital we don't allow this to get the better of us. Even highly successful people admit to feeling afraid when they step into unknown territory, but the difference between them and many others is they don't let this stop them.

As tempting as it can be to give in to our fears, it's important we resist this if we can. Giving in may relieve the pressure in that moment but it also strengthens our belief that we 'can't do it'. Our confidence shrinks, options close down and life becomes restricted. The best antidote to fear is taking action. Fear is overcome step by step, challenge by challenge, success by success. It's pointless to wait for our fears to subside before taking action because inactivity and avoidance usually heighten fear. What enables us to grow in competence and confidence and breaks the deadlock of fear is doing the things we are afraid of.

Sometimes taking action is just a matter of calling on our courage and moving forward boldly despite our apprehension, but at other times when our fears feel overwhelming we may need to find creative ways to support ourselves. Rather than reckless 'do or die' action we need considered, planned strategies that are likely to ensure a successful outcome. Each success leads to increased self-esteem and personal freedom and makes it easier to take the next step.

Fear can be generated by a harsh inner critic – comparing, judging, condemning, catastrophising, conjuring up memories of past difficulties and creating fear fantasies for the future. If we are anxious there is nothing to be gained by becoming self-critical. Adopting a bullying attitude towards ourselves will simply undermine our already shaky self-confidence. Just as a frightened child will become more distressed if treated harshly, so will we if we become hard on ourselves. Instead, when we feel afraid, we need to cultivate a gentle, comforting way of speaking to ourselves. Using encouraging self-talk will help considerably to calm our fears and increase our sense of personal power.

Usually it's important to take the time to acknowledge the extent of our worries and understand exactly what we are frightened of. Nameless, undefined fears can insidiously eat away at our confidence. When we know and accept our fears we are able to decide if they are realistic concerns or highly exaggerated fantasies. Our imagination can play tricks on us by creating alarming scenarios and this creates anxiety. We then begin to behave apprehensively and sometimes this helps to bring about the very thing we dreaded.

We can break this cycle by becoming aware of fear fantasies, looking at them objectively, challenging them or just deciding to let them go. We can build our confidence by actively remembering times when we have successfully conquered fear, bluffed our way through, been bold or handled a difficult situation well. It is useful to remember that we usually look far more self-assured than we feel and that most of the things people fear never happen. Realistic concerns can usually be overcome by practical strategies which help to boost us as we tackle the new challenge.

When we face our fears in these forthright ways, it is often surprising just how quickly we change. Before we know it, our comfort zone has expanded and we can easily accomplish tasks that previously had our heart racing and our stomach churning. Having mastered previously daunting situations we continue to encounter new ones. As humans we have a need to grow and challenge ourselves repeatedly. That means continuing to expand our comfort zone by testing ourselves out in new, often scary, situations. The stories of Judi Grace and Barbara Koziarski remind us of the wonderful feeling of satisfaction, pride and self-esteem we can experience when we challenge ourselves to take the risk of stepping out of our comfort zone, keep moving forward despite our fears, and emerge triumphant, having achieved what we set out to do.

Judi Grace

' . . .if you give out energy and warmth and generosity it comes back to you . . .'

Judi runs her own successful consultancy business offering training in strategic planning, assertiveness, interpersonal skills and team building. She also works as a one-to-one coach and mentor helping people to achieve their goals. Judi's quiet determination and courage have enabled her to overcome doubts, fears, health problems and financial hardship to achieve her dream of training and working in this field.

Judi went to Massey University as a solo parent and graduated in 1991 with a BA in psychology and a Diploma in Business Studies. She was offered work with Ansett after being there for a field study placement and over the following two years ran courses for all 1000 members of Ansett New Zealand's staff. She has gone on to develop a thriving business with a list of corporate clients and an income in the top one per cent for women in New Zealand. Her achievements were recognised in 1997 when she won the CLEAR Self-employed Woman of the Year award.

Judi believes strongly in the importance of giving to the community and encourages the people in her courses to do 'random acts of kindness'. She has been a Lifeline counsellor and has conducted many workshops in the community and prisons. She is currently a JP and a marriage celebrant. Judi has two sons and lives in Auckland with her partner Kiri Warburton. He shares her belief in giving back to the community.

Ten years ago I was on the Domestic Purposes Benefit. Now I work as a consultant inspiring others to be the best they can be and I love my work passionately. My mission is to live life fully and to empower others to believe in themselves. I believe for myself I can be anything I want to be. I came out of a violent marriage and I've made some huge changes since then and I needed to because I was a wuss. I wanted people to like me desperately, so I didn't say what I felt or thought. I thought that by saying nothing I'd keep the peace and I just suppressed my feelings. I've since learnt that's the wrong thing to do. For a start it did nothing for my health. I was full of seething resentment and I actually ended up getting cancer. Now I've learnt that it's important to say what you think and feel, as long as you do it diplomatically and tactfully. We can be gentle and firm and say our piece and we owe that to ourselves and the people we come into contact with.

These days I'm mostly assertive and empowered compared to what I used to be, and I'm looking forward to developing that even more. Occasionally I slip back into my old passive ways. I have doubts and I'm vulnerable but I've found sharing my vulnerability helps me bridge gaps with people and connect with them. Sometimes I still get scared when I'm asked to do things, but I just think, 'Oh damn it. I'm going to do it anyway,' although if it was way out of my league I'd ask for help.

Prior to my marriage break-up I was a very quiet little teacher. I'd sit in the staff room and listen but I wouldn't contribute a lot. I thought everyone had interesting lives except me. I was fine in the classroom, I could manage that, but whenever other adults were there or I took children away on school camps and had to get up and speak in front of parents, oh God that was challenging. I was so frightened that I'd make a fool of myself.

I'd been very shy all my life. I was a stoic, solidly built and scared little girl and I just sat and stared and I didn't offer much, the way I did in the staff room when I became a teacher. I just didn't think I had anything to contribute. I missed School Cert the first time and that does nothing for your confidence. When I was 19 I applied to do Volunteer Service Abroad, VSA, and I spent a year teaching in Fiji. That did show a bit of grit!

When I was married I had a dream of becoming a personnel con- sultant but I used to get heaps of put downs and emotional blackmail so I didn't feel confident. I thought I was dumb because that was what I was being told. My ex-husband used to scorn me for even thinking about going to university. I kept what was happening a big secret and pretended that everything was fine because I was actually very ashamed. The marriage ended after an awful episode of violence where I was a cowering, pathetic little heap in the corner and he just kicked the hell out of me. My youngest son was watching and crying from the doorway. That decided it for me. It was over.

A major turning point came for me when I went to assertiveness classes. I learned that it was alright to say what you think and that it was actually a useful thing to do. It was there that I took the huge step of voicing my dream to go to university. And no one laughed! That was a complete turn around from what I'd experienced in twelve years of marriage. When I said, 'I'd like to go to university,' and expected laughter or derision they actually went the other way and said, 'Well, why don't you?' It was the first time anyone had ever encouraged and challenged me about it. So I enrolled in just one paper.

When I first went to university it was scary. Just filling in the application form was hard. It was extramural so they'd send me all these books and papers and I'd sit there and think, 'I don't know what the hell to do with this.' The whole thing was way out of my comfort zone. Going down to my first vocation course in Palmerston North was like going into another world. There were people hungry for learning and I couldn't get enough of it. I'd talk to people and ask them about their courses and I heard people talking about these communication papers for a Diploma in Business Studies and it sounded so good. I was doing a BA so I went to the Dean and asked if I could cross credit some of my BA papers and do the diploma. He said, 'No you don't usually do a diploma at the same time as a BA,' and I said, 'What about if I put up a good case?' So I did and he agreed.

The most powerful thing was when I got my assignments back. In the beginning they came back with a C or a C^+, but once I started getting the hang of what they wanted they came back with A on them and every now and again A^+. I'd open up my mail and there would be an A^+ and I'd be so overwhelmed that someone thought I was clever that I'd just cry.

While I was studying I was working as well to help make ends meet. I used to clean people's houses during the day and proofread for the *New Zealand Herald* at night and my four-year-old son would be sleeping beside me in a sleeping bag. It was an awful time. I just raced from one task to another. I'd get up and do a couple of hours on assignments, take my son to kindy, go swimming, come home, do some more work on assignments, clean people's houses, go and pick him up from kindy and spend some time with him. I also took children for reading tuition after school. Then after dinner we'd go into the Herald and I'd proofread until one, two or three o'clock in the morning, come home, get up early and go through it all again. It was exhausting but in a way it was also quite helpful because it stopped me feeling sorry for myself. I think it's very easy to get into self-pity but I didn't have time for that.

Then I was diagnosed with cancer. I was just over halfway through my degree and in the middle of my exams. My first thought was, 'Chuck it in. I don't need this.' I was doing six papers and I didn't even have time for an operation. I had a crisis of confidence. It was very much, 'Why me? I don't deserve this. How come now when I'm doing so well?' And I did go into victim thoughts of, 'I'm not supposed to do this. Who do I think I am?' I remember lying on my bed and crying.

That's where the working hard was a coping mechanism. I'd become a Lifeline counsellor by then and I'd be driving to a Lifeline shift and thinking, 'Oh God, I don't have time for this. This is silly. I'm more disempowered that the people phoning in.' Then I'd pick up the phone and there'd be the perfect call for me. Sometimes I'd realise they were in the 'poor me' real victim mode and it was like, 'Oh wow! I've actually moved on from that,' so that was affirming. And I'd just put myself in their shoes, be absolutely empathetic, do a good call for forty minutes then put the phone down and think, 'Great.' As I drove home I'd feel really fortunate and I'd think, 'Wow, I am rich. I am OK.' That very much helped me to cope and keep going.

Every single week of my study I used to think, 'I can't do this. It's too hard. I'm going to give up.' It was usually over a stinking little assignment with a horrible topic that I just couldn't get my head around. So I'd leave it and go swimming and that helped to clear my head. Then I'd come back and look at the assignment again and think, 'I know what they want.'

What kept me going was the dream of going up on the stage and graduating. It was very powerful. I'd started learning about visualisation and I put it into practice. I could see myself wearing the black gown and hear the applause and feel the experience. I consciously worked at creating that image as a way of motivating myself. When things got really hard I'd think about my graduation – dream it – and it was like the light at the end of the black tunnel.

So my desire to graduate became stronger than my desire to chuck it in. It was also about trusting myself, because when I was a teacher if anything got too hard for me and I got anxious I could make myself sick. If ever there was a school inspector in the school I could bring about the flu or stomach pains. It was a coping mechanism. So the hanging in there to do the double degree was about changing that pattern, although I can only say that now. I didn't realise I was doing that at the time. I just knew it was important not to give up. After three lots of major surgery I was finally cleared of cancer. It was such a relief!

Visualising my graduation did have a powerful impact. I can feel the tears coming up as I remember it. That day when I graduated was very special because I went on stage in the morning and I got a BA and then I went up again in the afternoon and got a Diploma in Business Studies. I was so proud. It was probably the most powerful feeling I've ever had. I felt affirmed, like, 'Wow, I've got guts!' And I knew then I could handle anything that came my way. That was quite a revelation really and I've held on to that. Nothing is ever going to be that hard again. Every now and again when things get difficult I remind myself of that time and consciously use that memory to help me to feel stronger.

After I graduated I went and worked at Ansett New Zealand as their trainer. I had quite a bit of performance anxiety in those early days and there were many times when I wanted to give up. I was incredibly intimidated by handsome pilots and gorgeous-looking flight attendants and I'd give my power away. If I had some resistance from them I'd be thinking, 'I've got no right to be running this course. I'll just leave right now.' But I never ever did. When I got home and I'd be so tired and I'd have a little cry and say, 'I can't do this.' But the next day was another day, so that was fine. I'd keep going.

It's been life changing to discover that if you have a dream or a goal and you write it down and you think about it, you achieve it. My goals are written in my diary so I read them often. Some of my goals are really simple like 'I have an abundance of energy'. I write them as affirmations and it's like they become part of my being and everything I do is geared towards them because they are always in my presence.

As someone who's had cancer, self-care has been absolutely paramount. That's why the majority of my goals are around getting balance, eating well, sleeping well and spending time with my partner, family, friends and myself. There isn't anything more important. But it's a struggle sometimes because there are too many things to do and not enough time to do them. When people say, 'Can you do . . .' my inclination is to say, 'Yes.'

I know I have unrealistic expectations of myself at times. I think I can achieve everything. Sometimes it feels like it's been all work and not enough play. In the last three years with my new earned wealth I've been buying rental properties and I've just bought my eighth. That's been amazing, but it's also been quite a lot of work. Just to go through the whole buying procedure and lawyers and mortgage brokers and then to get them tenanted or to paint them up, which I often do myself – that's pushing it a bit. I constantly struggle with getting a balance. Recently when I was driving to my lawyer I just got in touch with, 'Judi, you're going off to sign up for your eighth rental property. Look at where you came from – the DPB. Wow!' and all of a sudden I was so overwhelmed I was crying. I felt incredibly grateful.

In 1999 I was invited by Massey University to be the guest speaker at the graduation ceremony. When the phone call came I was so emotional I just froze and actually couldn't get my breath. I felt overcome with joy and fear all wrapped up together and thought, 'Oh my God, not me! Why me? I can't do this.' But I said yes! In fact I was assertive. I said I'd think about it and I'd get back to them. I got off the phone and I thought, 'No bugger it, I'm doing it.'

When I told my partner Kiri he thought it was great. He just loves and believes in me and absolutely encourages me. Probably if I was on my own I'd have more anxiety attacks, but I feel very cherished by him. I was scared but I had three months and I prepared my speech really, really carefully. I know procrastination robs me of my feelings of empowerment. Things get bigger in my mind when I put them off so for me the important thing is to start. Once I'd started planning and had a framework on paper I found a lot of the fear went away.

And it went really well! A video was made of it and I do look really accomplished, but what they couldn't see was behind the lectern my knees were knocking. I was really scared, but to get up there and sit with all the professors was wonderful. I'd been in their classes and here I was with them and they were shaking my hand and saying, 'It's lovely to have you here.' Afterwards you do a walk around the town square in Palmerston North and the chancellor and the vice chancellor asked me to walk between them. So I marched down the road with them right in the front, behind the piper and I just thought, 'This feels magic!' It was overwhelming – it really was.

I have an incredible appreciation of what I have and the people I attract into my life. It's important to me to give back to the community. My parents have always been very generous in their contributions to the community. I'm a marriage celebrant and a Justice of the Peace and I was a Lifeline counsellor for eleven years. In the past I've run community workshops in communication skills and anger management. I wouldn't know any other way to live really. I believe if you give out energy and warmth and generosity it comes back to you, although that's not the reason for doing it. You do it because it's obviously a lot healthier, much more pleasant way to live. I've had a personal vision for the last five years: I want to leave my boys a legacy of good self-esteem, of overcoming the odds and of acceptance and optimism. That's what I want to role model to my sons. And that you don't just take, you've got to give back.

Judi's message

Share your dreams with someone who believes in you. Be selective about who you mix with. Develop friendships with people who are inspiring, encouraging and positive and let other friendships slide a little if those people drain you of energy. If you're dealing with fear you may need someone who believes in you and accepts you totally to work with you until you can do it on your own. It may be that you have to pay someone like a life coach to do that but make an investment and pay for resources that you need and be generous with yourself. You're worth it!

I believe the more we can build up our self-confidence and self-acceptance the better. I think it's really important to respect and accept yourself, then other people will too. I don't think we were put here to be critical of ourselves. That serves no purpose. So be kind and generous to yourself and others and let the perfectionism go. Do visualisations and affirmations and do things for other people because that helps you feel better about yourself. You'll always find someone who's more scared than you are. Be the best you can be. You owe it to yourself and to the universe.

Barbara Koziarski

'These days as women we're allowed to live our lives out loud and quite clearly we need to . . .'

Barbara is the founder of Presentations Consulting Ltd, a Wellington-based company offering practical assistance to people who need to make presentations to groups. Barbara developed the training aspect of the company because she saw a need for it. In 1995 Barbara had the idea of setting up 'The Speakers Gym', a communication circuit where women could go on a regular basis to practise their public speaking skills in a non-threatening environment. Over the years hundreds of women have taken advantage of this opportunity to benefit from Barbara's coaching, feedback and encouragement.

As preparation for her training role Barbara went looking for help from a variety of sources: presentation courses, aerobic dance and drama. However Barbara's main expertise in this area was earned through her own struggle to overcome self-doubt and fear. Barbara is able to offer the people she works with many insights and strategies from her personal experience, with the enthusiasm of one who is living life more boldly, and the humility of one who is still at times dealing with these issues. In effect Barbara's biggest challenge may well be her greatest gift.

I used to be shy and introverted and not be able to mingle with businesspeople and speak the language and stand up in front of people. When I managed to do things differently I'd get really excited about my success and say, 'Yes! I'm doing this well.' Now the thing that excites me is seeing my influence on the people I work with — seeing their success. That's what I'm passionate about. My vision is to have whatever skills, patience and words I need to enable those who come to me to reach their goals.

I grew the training part of the company for myself about seven years ago because clients would come and pick up the slides for their presentations and as they were leaving almost as an aside they'd say, 'I feel a bit nervous.' That mirrored the nervousness I felt at that time because I'd very quickly realised you can't run a successful presentations company unless you can do presentations successfully, and I felt nervous about that.

At that stage I had so many fears. I was afraid I didn't have the proper qualifications, that I'd be ridiculed or exposed as an impostor and of standing on my own two feet and taking responsibility for myself – that I was too old, too short, too dumb and too trivial. Somewhere I read 'If I show you who I am and you don't like me I have nothing else,' and that's how I felt. I knew I had to get over my fears because they were crippling me.

I was a shy, short, brainy, ordinary child. As I was growing up I was aware of others who were freer than me and I wanted to be like them and so that's what I've worked on. What I did a long time ago was personify fear as The Bastard Troll, the one that waits under the bridge to get me. I came to see it as a straight-out battle between how I want to live my life and The Bastard Troll who's out to stop me. It would say to me, 'You're not good enough. There will be somebody there who will know more than you. What you have to say is not worthwhile.' Once I saw it like that I knew I needed to arm myself with better strategies and a better game plan to diminish and weaken the grip of that fear. Then I could reply, 'I'm onto you. I know all your tricks, but I'm smarter than you.'

I've worked on my fears in different ways. I attacked them like a problem that needed a solution, and I did it practically and sensibly. I wasn't satisfied with the way things were so I thought, 'That way looks better. I want it. How do I go about getting it?' I think the essential part was to say, 'This is where I am and it dissatisfies me. They look like they're having a whole heap of fun over there. If I watch very carefully and have a bit of a practice I can look like I'm one of them and inch my way over and sneak in subtly disguised as one of them, and then I can have what they're having,' and that's what I did. I pushed myself and practised and sometimes bombed, but when I did I picked myself up and reviewed what happened and revised my strategies and tried again.

I realised I'd been collecting evidence of failures, telling myself, 'I can't do this because . . .' and sometimes they were old failure messages from a long time ago. To overcome my doubts and fears I started to look for and collect evidence of my success when I spoke publicly. So I'd watch to see how people were responding and notice a nod or a comment. Sometimes people would come up afterwards and say, 'You really spoke to me. That touched me,' and I'd go home and write that down. So I started to think that I was worthwhile because I had proof of it. And once I could shore myself up with that external proof I got better at not needing it.

About six years ago I thought I'd like to pass on what I'd learnt, so I decided to set up a clinic and invite the people of Wellington to come and ask me whatever they wanted to about giving presentations. I started off in a very small way with eight women, including my niece and our cleaning woman to boost the numbers, and I told them everything I'd learnt in the previous couple of weeks. Since then it's really grown with more than 600 women benefiting from the Speaker's Gym sessions. The women build their confidence by physically practising the skills of speaking in a group and it's extremely satisfying to see the change in them.

Working with that particular group is a way for me to put something back into the community, which is what I was raised to do. When I'm working with these women it reminds me of how terrified I used to be. I'd go to a networking event or a social event with my husband and I'd stand outside the men's toilets and wait until he came out so I could be with him. The idea of being left or joining a group and talking to people absolutely terrified me. So I understand fear and I'm sometimes still dealing with my self-doubt on a minute by minute basis. That's what people find inspiring. If I can stand up and speak without notes it gives them great hope that it's also within their range.

The French writer Émile Zola said, 'If you asked me what I came into this world to do I would tell you that I came to live my life out loud.' I quite like that, but it's a paradox because we were raised in a Methodist background — three quiet girls — and the idea of living your life out loud was not what you did. These days as women we're allowed to live our lives out loud and quite clearly we need to, especially in business. It's not an option really, it's a necessity. For the women I work with it's often a matter of undoing a whole lot of stuff that's inappropriate and not required on the journey. We've got to get rid of any old limiting messages and break those taboos; those messages about keeping a low profile and not showing off. When I was a child, showing off was one of the worst things you could do. So how you get over it is to say, 'My work requires me to have this set of skills, one of which is an ability to communicate to a group. If I'm not able to do this then I'm not doing my work.'

People come to me because they want to speak not only to big gatherings but in team meetings or they want to have influence at their work. I think it's normal to have fears and we need to develop robust coping strategies, so I help people to make their fears quite specific and work out strategies to combat and counteract those fears. Then I say to them, 'Do your work' and that's quite grounding for them, because they're paid to do a job and their job description says, 'excellent oral communication skills' so they have to do their work. I think that reminds them of what they're really there for.

I've found in the work that I do that most people have an invisible sign around their neck saying 'Did I do alright? Am I OK? Did you like me?' It's not actually said but it's a subtext. My answer to this question is, 'Yes. I believe in you strongly and your worth has nothing to do with your failure or your success in this particular task.' Because until we can get that internal locus of approval we need a bit of affirmation from others.

I've learned when you're speaking to groups you have to take the ego out of it. I've got to the stage now that I say to myself, 'It's not all about you, you know.' I also say that to the chairman of the board or the board members or whoever I'm working with. A wise colleague told me that before she stands up to speak to a group she thinks, 'Who am I for this group today?' so that's something I ask myself and that really helps.

Before I work with people I'll often prepare myself by saying, 'Grant me the wisdom to do or say the right things for this particular person,' or 'Grant me the stillness I need for this particular task.' I'm saying, 'If I'm the conduit for the message, pass it through me now and grant me whatever skills I need to enable me to do this work.' That's only come from a process of thinking less about me and more about my audience.

I'm greatly sustained by the work that I do. I find it enormously satisfying. For years I lived life the hard way – the repressed, stifled, worried, 'beat yourself up' way. Now I've learned the easy way – the 'have a go', liberated, 'don't worry about it too much' way, and I find the easy way is so much better. I've learnt the world's a far more forgiving, accepting place than I thought. If you're a perfectionist riddled full of self-doubts you will think that everybody is judging, condemning or ridiculing, when in fact they're nodding with encouragement, identifying or saying, 'God I wish I could be like her.'

I'd like to get to the stage where I don't have a dialogue of self-doubt going on inside me, but if I permanently triumphed over self-doubt I don't think I'd have the same humility to enable me to work with others. I've come a long way – from being really fearful to the point where I can say, 'I am the way I am. I look the way I look. I am my age.' For many years of my life I was closed and shy. I'd much rather live my life out loud.

Barbara's message

Your dream doesn't have to be earth-shattering but you can live your life more fully without regret. Don't care about any rules that say you can't have your dream because it's an inappropriate dream or it's too big for you. Even if you can't realise your dream in the shape that it is in your head at the moment, don't let that stop you. Do something towards it and your dream may adjust as you go. Most people's dreams start with a step. My mother used to say, 'If you want something to happen, start it!' So just begin any old where and see where it goes. Some kind of action is more satisfying than having the dream unrealised because you couldn't begin it.

To overcome self-doubt and fear you need to look for and collect evidence of your success: people accepting you and your leadership skills, people laughing at your humour and giving you positive feedback. Write these things down and then say them to yourself in the present context and say, 'Hey I'm good at this.' That way you'll gradually come to accept that those things are true. It's not like a wish list or pumping yourself up because these things are actually true about you. It's just helping you to believe that. So collect evidence of your successes and become bolder and it will change your life.

MEETING
THE CHALLENGE
OF SETBACKS

When you look at life and its many challenges as a test, you begin to see each issue you face as an opportunity to grow . . .

Don't Sweat the Small Stuff, Richard Carlson

When we set our sights on a goal and begin to move forward, our resolve is usually challenged by unexpected setbacks. Often the bigger our aspirations, the bigger the potential obstacles. If we view this as part of the process of achievement we are less likely to be thrown by it. Every time we hit an obstacle or difficulty we have a choice: we can become immobilised and give up or rise to the challenge by re-evaluating, reorganising and proceeding. The decision is ours.

Setbacks can be a gift, although it may not feel like it at the time. They often bring out the best in us by forcing us to renew our commitment and strengthen our resolve to continue to pursue our goals. They challenge us to think creatively about our problems and come up with smart solutions, which frequently lead to an even better outcome.

When we are confronted by an obstacle it is vital to maintain our optimism. The old saying 'where there's a will there's a way' is a wonderfully empowering belief to hold in the face of adversity. We can bring our determination to bear by looking past the obstacle and keeping our sights firmly on our goal. This helps to keep the situation in perspective and remind us that this setback is simply an inconvenience on the path that we will one day look back on.

If, when we encounter a setback, we allow ourselves to feel defeated and lament, 'Why me?', we render ourselves powerless. If instead we ask the questions, 'What can I do to improve the situation?

How can I overcome this? What is the best way to move forward?', we empower ourselves and engage our creative mind in the search for a solution. We may not discover an instant answer but we open ourselves to the possibilities. It's amazing how, when we approach setbacks in this way, a perfect idea often pops into our mind, sometimes when we are not even focusing on the challenging situation.

When we feel blocked by a setback we need to make a plan of action and keep moving forward, however slowly. Certain obstacles may seem insurmountable at first glance but they rarely are. Even in the worst of situations there is usually a way to proceed. If one path is blocked we can usually choose another and very often when we do, new opportunities open up. As we maintain our focus and proceed as best we can, our tenacity is likely to be rewarded. Frequently obstacles can be overcome in the most surprising ways by a turn of events we would never have imagined. We come across important new information or the difficult circumstance suddenly changes. It's as if when we are fully committed, life moves to support us. The important thing is not to allow a setback to stop us in our tracks because inactivity creates a sense of defeat. As we keep moving forward we summon our determination to succeed.

Many wonderful achievements have been made by people who suffered setbacks and 'failures'. Keri Hulme was refused by numerous publishers before her book *The Bone People* was accepted for publication and went on to win the prestigious Booker Prize. When Wendy Pye was made redundant unexpectedly, she turned this to her advantage by going on to establish her own publishing company. She is now New Zealand's wealthiest woman. Barbara Kendall's windsurfing career was jeopardised after her arm was slashed by a boat propeller, yet she went on to win a gold medal in the Olympics a few months later. These women found the inner strength to persist. If they had allowed setbacks to get the better of them their stories would have been very different.

When obstacles are threatening to overwhelm us, it is time to focus on our goal and draw on our belief in our resilience and our faith that eventually this tough time will pass and we will achieve what we set out to do. The power of determination, tenacity and passion to overcome obstacles is well demonstrated in the following stories shared by Jill Mitchell and Kapka Kassabova.

Jill Mitchell

'We're all here together but each of us has to inspire ourselves. We can't wait for someone else to do it.'

Jill is the founder and Managing Director of Wild Daisies Publications, a company she created in 1996 to publish her own range of children's books and educational aids. Jill's company came about as a result of a dream she had for many years to write and illustrate a range of vibrant and exciting readers which would enable children to develop their self-esteem while learning to read.

In need of a career change at 48, Jill drew on her natural talent for art, her experience as a teacher and her delight in nature to create a truly inspiring range of readers which feature five fabulous frog characters. Zip, Zeek, Zak, Zo and Zoosh capture the imagination of her young readers while instilling life skills and values. Jill's books have been well received. Of the 3500 primary schools in New Zealand, 1700 of them have purchased her books for full reading programmes, reading recovery or special needs children.

It has taken an enormous amount of dedication to succeed in bringing her dreams into being without any initial funds, but Jill's focus, enthusiasm and commitment have carried her through the challenges and setbacks she has encountered. Jill operates her business from her home, Alva Cottage, in Ramarama south of Auckland. She has three adult children.

For a long time I'd had a huge desire to write and illustrate children's books that were colourful and exciting – adventures, a bit of mud, some caves, waterfalls and humour. As a teacher I'd worked with a lot with children who came from homes that were really, really dysfunctional. Nothing and nobody stayed the same for them and they didn't even try to make friends because they shifted so often. I wanted to put companionship and friendship into these books for them.

I'd always had a natural gift for art but I'd never used it, although I felt really strongly that I should. The opportunity came after I slid down the wall teaching. I'd actually collapsed a couple of times and landed up in hospital and been severely warned that I had high blood pressure and I was right on the edge of a stroke or a heart attack. The doctors at the hospital told me very strongly, 'Do something about it or you may not get another chance,' and I lay in hospital and thought, 'Oh my goodness, if I have a stroke that's me. I've had it.' That terrified me.

Three weeks later at the end of the term I left teaching. I had my holiday pay and no savings at all. I'd come through a marriage break-up three and a half years before and had only just been able to buy my own house and the mortgage was huge. I didn't know how I'd manage financially but two of my kids came home between flats with their partners, cats and dogs. That was good because they paid board and that gave me five months until they sorted themselves and left again.

So I began to get up early and write and draw in the woodshed, which was just an open lean-to, then go and do children's reading recovery for an hour and a half in the morning and work on way into the night. I've always been fascinated by frogs and very quickly the first frog character came in. By the time my children left I couldn't bear to stop so I decided to rent out my house and go house sitting and the rent paid the mortgage. I found the houses either by word of mouth or advertising in the little local papers. It was a stressful time for me in some ways. I can remember coming out in this terrible rash from head to toe that just itched me to death. It lasted for two or three months. I realise now it was nerves.

At first I had no idea that I'd end up publishing the books myself. I ran them past several educational publishers and although they liked what they saw, nobody would pick up the twenty-four books I'd decided were necessary to bring in twenty-three basic words the kids needed to learn to read and write. And nobody would let me illustrate them so I just took them straight back, because there was no way someone else could illustrate them when they were already in my head. I just couldn't bear that. It's funny, the fact of money never entered the equation.

I didn't share my idea to write children's books with other people because I didn't want anyone to say, 'You must be mad if you think you can do that.' I was very, very vulnerable at that stage. So I stayed totally away from the world and moved around from house to house and only Mum and my kids and a select few knew where I was. Mack, my Labrador, came with me and I walked him twice a day around the cliffs and beaches and I just worked the strangest hours. It was fabulous in that way. I had $16 a week over after I paid my mortgage and no savings so I actually got really thin during that time. Mack and I were eating a lot of rice and I was getting great work done. I'd just sleep, wake up, work, take Mack for a walk and it didn't matter what time of the day or night it was.

Eventually I got to the stage where I just knew I couldn't keep living on $16 dollars a week. I can't remember how, but I somehow got to the Methodist Mission and they got me to do this little business plan. I had no training in the business world and this elderly guy who spoke to me must have been totally amazed at what I thought I could do and what I'd done for my business plan, but he was very, very nice. By then I wanted to publish my books myself and I needed a huge amount of money — $58,000. I had no background in art or printing or marketing. He pointed me off to the Franklin Enterprise Agency and a couple of weeks later I went and talked to them. By then I was feeling terribly vulnerable because I was getting skinny. They said, 'Look what you're doing. You can't keep doing this. But look what you're creating. You have to keep going now. You're getting yourself into a new position to go forward in life. Go on the dole for a while,' and I thought, 'I can't do that.' It had just never even entered my head.

Three weeks later when I stood in that queue it was one of the hardest things I'd ever done. I kept thinking, 'I shouldn't be here,' but I knew I had to do something. I had to beg, plead and just about crawl to get on a benefit because I spoke like I could get a job tomorrow. I had a house of my own which I was desperate to hold on to because I'd had a terrific struggle to find one cheap enough to buy. I did get accepted because I had the doctor's letters to support me. Even now it gives me shudders down my back every time I drive past that place, but it was the best thing that ever happened because it qualified me to do a small business course.

I was still house sitting and doing my books and I did this fantastic course that lasted six weeks and they brought in accountants and bank managers, they taught us to do cash flow charts – everything. All these things that I'd never even heard of in the teaching world. So then I had an idea of how to run a little business, which was amazing. I just loved it, but I was still not brilliant at figures.

About that same time I happened to meet one of the neighbours through a fence where I was house sitting. I was untangling Mack who was barking at him and he wondered who I was. He came over to introduce himself and I had these pictures all over the lounge drying and he was very interested and listened to all my hopes and dreams. A few months later Wayne came in as my business partner. He's an accountant and he was able to raise the money we needed to do that initial lot of printing. My house went on the line and still is, but by then I was so committed I could never have turned away from it.

It's worked out perfectly. Wayne works full time so I had to get the business off the ground and sell the books but I've never regretted that because it gave me the opportunity I needed. After nearly ten months I was able to go back home and my joy was reflected in seeing Mack galloping around his old haunts like a pup. It had been a long time wandering around.

Finding out about typesetting and printing was a challenge. I tried seven typesetters and I was beginning to despair because I couldn't get somebody suitable. I'd tell them what I'd wanted and they'd bring up on the computer screen what they thought I should have. The eighth guy finally listened to me and he was actually on the same beam so that was marvellous.

It was really important to me that the books were absolutely right.

When the printers were working on them there were times when I'd say, 'Yeah that's fine,' and then I'd drive down the road and I'd think, 'No! It's not bright enough,' and I'd go back and say, 'Stop!' I remember looking at the printer's face and knowing he was thinking, 'Oh my God, we've got one of these,' but the cost was on us so we'd dump that lot and start again. It was terrifying when the money was so tight.

When I first saw my books in print it was wonderful, but I was so tired it wasn't quite the euphoric moment you'd think it would be. There was also one major problem. Being a teacher I'd been really fanatical about getting the spacing between the words right, but when the books came out the words were too close together. I was so shocked because I'd checked that so carefully. It was too late to do anything about it because the opening was the next day. I couldn't tell anyone. I had to get up there, sell those books and tell people they were fabulous and agonise quietly over it.

So that was a very bad few weeks, but we sold a lot of books. I kept really good track of who bought them and then after we'd been going about three months we reprinted them and replaced those books. Of course that put us further in debt but it had to be done. It was just one of those things – but it was a pretty major one.

A month after we got the books out I took them to the Frankfurt Book Fair. I still find that hard to believe because it's the biggest book fair in the world and I'd never even been to a fair before. There wasn't even time to be nervous. I had no idea what to expect so I just blew up pictures from the books on the photocopier and laminated them. I had this big stack of things and Blu-Tack and double sided tape and it worked really well. The stand looked lovely.

It was funny because it was another one of those things that eventually just fell together. At the last minute of the fair, this guy from Australia came up and he wanted me to distribute his books in New Zealand. I brought them back to look at them, then I thought, 'No, there's no way we can do this. I'm still working on how we do it for ourselves.' So I contacted him and told him and that's when he said,

'Well who's got yours in Australia?' So he picked mine up and they've sold well there.

I'd decided I'd only sell the books to schools because kids need something new when they get to school. When I was teaching it used to break my heart every time I got a group of little new entrants and they'd be all ready to learn to read and I'd pull out the books and they'd say, 'I've seen that at kindy,' or 'I've got that at home.' You'd lost that magic moment and you never quite got it back again. So I just always knew that I'd never sell my books so the kids got to see them before they got to school. It would be so easy to and it would be good money wise, but money is not one of my major reasons for doing this.

It took sixteen months to go from creating the first twenty-four books in the woodshed to starting to sell them into the schools. Another teacher and I were the first reps out there and that was a terrifying time because we were putting them in front of teachers, but we did get a good response. I also ran the office for eighteen months but I soon realised that every time I was in the office or packing books or trying to get the records straight, the books weren't getting sold. I knew I had to get more reps, so I advertised in the local newspapers around the North Island, then I drove around in my little old van and my 83-year-old mother came with me. I interviewed people and got about five to sell on a commission-only basis. I did the same round the South Island in the Christmas holidays, travelling by train with my sister and we've boxed along ever since with eleven or twelve reps.

Because of the type of job we've got there's no income from November to March. I've thought of selling the house when we've got really tight because it can be a pretty long haul at times. With everything relying on me I think I'd have gone mad if I thought about it too much. There have often been bills to pay and no money and I've learned to think, 'OK, this is Friday night. Nothing can happen until Monday morning. I needn't worry about it until then.' And if things get stressful I lie in the bath with music and oils at any hour of the day or night. Lovely!

I've done every job in the business. Whatever has needed to be done I've just learned as I've gone along but I've got help in the office now and I work with two other artists, Geoffrey Cox and Jo Bridge. Jo's like me, not trained but we've got natural ability. We are so in tune I can draw something, we'll sit and talk about it and Jo goes away and draws it and brings it back and I feel like I've done it and Jo says it's like she hasn't done it at all. So it's really strange how it works. We get on wonderfully well because we've got no rules to break. We mix everything together and it works. So that's terrific!

I used to work a lot in the middle of the night, sleep a few hours then get up and work again. When I had to do the business and the art I found it so hard to make that transition from my business to my arty self. Then to my absolute surprise I realised I was doing both without even thinking about it. I'd be working on the accounts and then I'd turn around and draw something. I didn't think I could do that but I had to learn to because it was necessary. I can draw anything, anywhere, at any time now.

I really want my books in every reading programme in New Zealand schools because they work so well and they're fun and because the characters are a group of friends who go through with the reader as they're learning. The kids usually read each of those books at least five times so they know these frogs so well and they pick up on the caring and sharing and positive values and life skills in these books.

I also want these books to be all over the world. I've written my vision for where they're going on my office wall. I see them being in ghettos and little shacks and high rise apartments. They'll not just be in the middle of the road schools in America, they'll be giving a lot of joy and hope in war torn places where people are trying to put their lives back together. I've recently been contacted by a guy who's dealing with a request from the World Bank and the United Nations for reading books for East Timor. Our books are being assessed now. That was a wonderful request – totally out of the blue.

My childhood has had a huge influence on my work. I grew up on a dairy farm and I was allowed to keep frogs in my bedroom. I loved the farm life and the streams and trees, animals and birds. I was a kid who couldn't wait for the bell to go at school to get outside. Children just love nature but a lot of children are never, ever shown it – a trail of ants carrying a dead bumblebee home and how they're all helping each other or acorns or reflections on the water upside down. I had parents who showed me those sorts of things so I was fortunate and I wanted to share that world that is invisible to some people.

I get my inspiration from nature. If I'm feeling a bit tired or have no ideas, I just wander down to the stream and look at the things you don't normally see. It may just be the colour through the leaves or the shape of the reflection shining up the bank and I come back full of so many ideas. Sometimes I actually have to go, 'Stop, stop, stop. No more! I've got to get this lot down first,' because the ideas are coming in bang, bang, bang. I love it! It's been like that all the way along but I find it easier to access now than I ever have before. I don't question the ideas I get anymore. I just go with them.

After twenty years of bringing up a family and being really busy I actually lost track of who I was and I lost my appreciation for nature for quite a while. I didn't see any of those things anymore. I was in a really bad state before I walked away from my marriage. I'd got locked into this world of coping. It was a really quite desperate feeling but it was nobody's fault. It just was something that happened. It took me four years, without realising it, to get strong enough to walk away because it just broke my heart. With three teenagers it was a terrible time to leave but I just knew if I didn't all of us would go down the tubes. That was eleven years ago now, although it's been hard it was definitely the right thing to do.

I'm much freer and more creative now and my intuition is part of my life and I live totally by it. One thing I'm still learning to do is to let things flow and not try to stop them because things work out so beautifully once you let them. I've got a most unlikely friend I met quite by chance about three years ago, a very interesting guy. Malcolm lives in America, travels a lot and collects art and he used to work for NASA. He's had a wonderful influence on my life and I've really learnt not to assume or presume about as many things as possible, because you just never know. He's quite a lot older than me, and a very gentle soul. He's been here twice and he watches what happens and never says very much.

The last time he was here I didn't know what was wrong with me but I was restless and I knew I needed to get somewhere to work. Malcolm had seen me working in the woodshed the year before but I couldn't leave anything in there overnight because snails went in and ate all the paper. I don't mind roughing things for a while but it wasn't working for me anymore, so I decided to knock a wall out and build in the woodshed in a really basic way, just using what we had. We were creating an area that would have been really difficult to work in, but it would have been better than nothing.

Malcolm was just floating around saying nothing much at this stage but when he left he wrote me a cheque and said, 'You're not doing anything creative. You're dying. Do the studio properly.' I was totally blown away. It was quite hard for me to take the money because I've always said, 'I can do this.' Perhaps one day I'll give it back to him. He'll be absolutely delighted to see what I'm doing. We've created this wonderful studio and as soon as it started to go together I could see the whole next leap of my life.

I'm definitely a spiritual person but I'm not into religion. I had a big confusion about this for a long time because I grew up with a mum who took us to church and I always hated it. As a shy young child I even argued with the Sunday school teacher about angels on clouds. As I've got older I've realised that really that's got nothing to do with the spiritual side of people. The churches do what they like, but the spiritual side is totally free and open and I'm really comfortable with that.

I realise now I've got a lot of vision. I've discovered things unfold in their own time as long as you take the opportunities as they pass by. I think they're passing us by every instant of the day, often in disguise. I've certainly learned that the goals you write down happen. I've always been a really positive thinking person. I have to look for the best in things. I just can't bear not to. I love where I am in my life now at 53, because things that I've been puzzled about are actually starting to make sense.

I believe that each of us is solely responsible for the expansion of our own mind and the enchantment of our own imagination, but it's fun to share. We're all here together but each one of us has to inspire ourselves. We can't wait for somebody else to do it. We must do with our life the best we can. I want to live a life where when I'm gone, I've left something behind that's going to make a difference to other people's lives. I want to put books out there that help children who are growing up in places that are difficult for them. If they can read stories that inspire them it gives them choices and the opportunity to absorb material that will change their lives. I have a huge passion about that. If I go from this life and there's people left behind enjoying my books, I'll be absolutely delighted.

Jill's message

You probably know where you want to go but your goal might be a million miles out in front of you and you've got no idea how you're going to get there. That was how it was for me. I didn't know how I was going to do the things I needed to do or get the money I needed, but it did work out because I had a vision and I kept going. If you write your goal down and then come back to what's right in front of you and do the first step and don't worry about how you're going to get there, it will work out for you too. Just keep moving ahead. It doesn't matter if you zigzag all over the place as long as you keep going. There are people out there doing incredible things who have done just that. Start in the woodshed if there's nowhere else to start or on the kitchen table — anywhere. Don't let that put you off. It's worth it to follow your dream! It's a wonderful feeling to be doing something that you really want to do.

Kapka Kassabova

'I think often you find yourself, or the place where you belong, by going through some kind of crisis.'

Kapka has written two volumes of poetry and two novels. The strength and depth of her writing have earned her critical acclaim. She was the winner of the best first book of poetry in the Montana Book Awards in 1998, a finalist for the best book of fiction in the Montana Book Awards in 1999, the joint winner of the 1999 Buddle Findlay Sargeson Fellowship and the winner of the 2000 Commonwealth Writer's Prize for the best first book in Southeast Asia and the South Pacific. These achievements are all the more remarkable because English is her fourth language, a language she has been speaking for less than ten years.

Kapka was born in Sofia, the capital of Bulgaria, in 1973. The family lived modestly in a one-bedroom flat in an apartment block. Kapka dreamed of being a writer and from the age of 15 had work published in Bulgaria. After the end of communism the family lived in England for a year but were unable to stay because Kapka was refused a visa by the British Home Office due to red tape. Instead the family moved to Dunedin and her father took up a lectureship at Otago University. In her initial years in New Zealand, Kapka experienced a sense of alienation and dislocation and longed to express herself through her writing but before she could she first had to master the English language, a task she has clearly achieved.

My writing gives me most things, more so as time goes by. Writing defines me, or rather I define myself through my writing. It gives me a sense of direction which I wouldn't have if I was doing anything else. It gives me a sense of meaning which likewise I can't imagine getting out of any other activity. It gives me a sense of purpose and I feel as though I'm doing the right thing, the thing that I was designed to do, if you like. For me language is very important. I have this need to articulate what appears to me to be a shapeless and chaotic universe and through writing make sense of it. And hopefully I help make sense of it for other people too.

It is when I write that I feel I'm actually living. I suppose a lot of people would perceive my lifestyle as exceedingly solitary because I write at home, but that's the way I want it to be. That suits me fine so I don't regard it as a sacrifice, or even a concession. I have quite a lot of positive constructive energy, but I think at the core of my overall optimism there is always an anxiety, some kind of apprehension about how things can suddenly go wrong quite inexplicably. I am motivated by a constant awareness of precious things and time ticking away. We don't have an unlimited amount of time or energy and it's essential for me to feel like I'm achieving something, but not just doing anything. I don't believe in just filling my life. There is a particular thing that I want to do and I wouldn't settle for anything else – the creative endeavor of writing.

I think there are two main reasons for my interest in writing. One is entirely personal, in other words it's to do with who I am and my personality, my temperament and my imagination, my constant hunger for something other than our immediate reality, which is something that I've always had. My writing satisfies those needs. The other reason is to do with my surroundings. I grew up in a very ugly part of Sofia, the capital of Bulgaria. It was just a concrete jungle to use a cliché, nothing but concrete blocks of flats and mud that went on for miles and miles. From very early on I was conscious of the ugliness and I needed some kind of alternative escape which I found in books and writing. My first conscious memory of writing is around 8, when I was writing poetry. At that time I was also discovering books and alternative worlds and that was a turning point for me.

I was a very self-absorbed, serious child and a very anxious, tearful adolescent. My family were extremely supportive so I had the best possible environment in that respect. My parents believed in me and my sister and unconditionally supported us. They truly defined for me the concept of unconditional love. They had the ability to be able to say, 'Whatever you do in your life I'll be behind you because I believe in you. Whatever makes you happy makes me happy.' So in that sense I can't speak enough about the support and the belief that my parents have had in me.

Of course growing up in a communist society confronts you with certain things that leave a mark on you, probably without you even realising. Although it can equip you with skills and a certain kind of resilience and toughness that you, growing up in democratic societies, will never have, it can also traumatise you. In a society like that there are very deep divisions that are invisible, at least at first glance. There are those who support the regime and those who don't. Of course if you openly oppose the regime you are in serious trouble and although my parents didn't, I knew how they felt about it and that naturally affected me. At school there were divisions, the kids of the party factions and the kids of the intellectuals, despicable because they were not aligned with the party. As I was from a family which belonged to the technological intelligentsia, I was regarded with suspicion by kids whose fathers were big bosses. As a result of this imposed order I went right to the other end of the spectrum and became an extreme individualist.

As a child I remember wanting to be a writer when I grew up but this kind of dream fluctuated throughout the years. I think there's always that degree of chance or circumstance which determines how we turn out professionally and I think in my case circumstances were on my side when it came to choosing a writing career. But of course you do have to be attuned to those circumstances and you have to be able to grasp them. So I don't know how much was just my personal determination and how much external factors.

When I was about 13 I was involved in my piano playing. My piano teacher, who was an important person in my life, was determined that I should be a pianist so I was influenced by that. She provided my first glimpse into the artistic world. Because my parents were in the technological intelligentsia they didn't mix with artistic people, and my piano teacher was from a different realm altogether. She was a very quirky person – very original, very brave. She was single and quite a tortured soul and she believed in me so strongly. That gave me the first indication that I could one day belong to the world of artists – to the world of art in general – so that was essential to my self-belief.

At that stage I went through quite a crucial experience that probably pushed me more in the direction of introspection and of course introspection led me to writing. I became very ill and I spent some time in hospital and I was quite severely disabled for a few months. As a result I had to stop playing the piano for quite a long time. So that was the end of my musical fantasies. I was in a critical condition and as I emerged from it I realised that it had been a blow to my musical career and naturally I was upset. But during that time in hospital and in convalescence afterwards I was reading a lot and writing poetry as well. I'd discovered that this was the only way for me to escape from something that I found very difficult to cope with. And at that time my grandmother, who was incredibly important to me, died so that amalgamated the whole thing.

I was first published when I was 15 and then through until the time when we left Bulgaria. So I was beginning to take myself seriously, but quite tentatively. I wasn't quite sure whether I could really be a writer, whether I was good enough. It was my dream but I always thought I'd be a writer on the side but in my real life I'd be an interpreter or a translator or a lecturer.

I was 18 when we came to New Zealand. Even though we were in a privileged position because my father was a senior lecturer at Otago University, the family struggled with the change. It was a matter of finding our feet – basically psychological and emotional survival. It was an intensely trying time for our whole family but for me it was a serious crisis which lasted about four years. I retreated within myself and isolated myself from an environment that I couldn't accept and I went through a very intense time of mind and soul searching. It was much more than a culture shock. It was a spiritual crisis. By that I mean a crisis at the deepest level of myself – a crisis of identity, of self, of meaning.

I discovered at one point during that time that I missed writing. In fact my distress could only be soothed through writing. I needed to find a way to express myself. I am one of those people who are not very good at bottling up things. I need some kind of creative expression otherwise I just fade and feel unwell.

Writing was a problem because I wasn't confident enough to write in English then. I was fluent but my language skills were not sophisticated and I had no experience of writing in English. I couldn't write in Bulgarian either because who would read what I wrote? I wasn't one of those closet poets. I wanted to communicate through my writing and how do you do that in a foreign language? So for a while this was the dilemma I had – and it was a torment.

During that time I developed depression and an eating disorder and agoraphobia. For a while I turned to painting because in painting you don't need language. That was very satisfying, very therapeutic. I had some therapy and that was definitely crucial to me. The psychiatrist said, 'Just believe in yourself and don't give in to fear.' That was very important. I needed to be told that. I think ultimately my recovery was simply due to my determination to pull myself out of it. I refused to become a victim of my circumstance or my weakness. I quite consciously decided that it was not worth it.

I had this kind of obsession or passion for learning new vocabulary, so wherever I lived the walls in my room would be covered with pieces of paper with words. I would have a few hours every week where I would sit down and look at the new words to try to memorise them, put them into context and so on. That was something I did for a long time because I was always terrified of not being able to convey my thoughts.

Gradually I gained the confidence to first translate some of my poetry from Bulgarian and then write straight into English. Later on I did a creative writing course at Victoria University. That gave me the opportunity to write full time for a few months. It was a test for me to see if I could stick it out without being sidetracked. I wrote my first novel largely during that time and I've been writing since then. During the previous four years that I had been in New Zealand I had written short stories, prose and of course poetry. At that time I also had my first book of poetry published, *All roads lead to the sea*.

Some people have said that my writing reads as though it's a translation from another language, which sometimes alarms me because I don't want that. I had my formative years in an East European culture rather than here, so that will always be part of me and the way I express myself. Sometimes I have to stop and think 'Hang on, am I expressing myself here in a way that is comprehensible to my English-speaking audience? Am I pitching this correctly? Am I going to be obscure or extravagant when I want to be precise?' It's not simply to do with language and vocabulary. You can acquire a gigantic vocabulary in a new language and still use it in odd ways, which I sometimes do. Being stuck in the middle of a sentence without the right word still haunts me to this day. I still have problems expressing myself in English, especially verbally. On the page I have time to think and come up with various options, but in speech I often find myself stumbling and groping for the right word. It can be terribly frustrating.

That crisis was a transitional time, but it felt like the end. In hindsight I understand it was part of the experience of being a new immigrant. It was the most serious thing I've had to overcome, far more serious than my illness when I was younger, or any other loss I'd been through. Because in a way I lost part of myself during that time of emotional struggle and at the same time I grew into someone new. I think that time was both a curse and a gift because it was quite horrifying but at the same time I wouldn't be the same person if I hadn't gone through it so I have gained something from it. I think often you find yourself, or the place where you belong, by going through some kind of crisis. It doesn't have to take a dramatic form like it did with me, it can simply be some kind of re-evaluation or self-questioning, but I don't think change happens painlessly or smoothly. I suppose the most enduring effect it's had on me is the knowledge that I can overcome most things, that very few things are fatal and final, and no matter how low you feel it's probably temporary. I think that's very important knowledge to have. I have emerged from that time much happier.

Kapka's message

I think fear is most often the obstacle to people taking that step towards their dream and it's vital to combat that. I can only say to others what I have said to myself at the critical time I went through. The worst thing to live with is fear, and as a result, regret for the things you haven't done because you feared them. I think for me, personally I want to avoid at any cost being motivated by fear. Therefore taking a risk is definitely worth it. If you don't risk something there's a 100 per cent chance you won't succeed, but if you do take a risk there is at least a 50 per cent chance that you will. So even statistically speaking it's worth it. And also I think a life without that sense of the unknown or adventure is really not worth living.

The most important thing is to maintain a level of quality and excellence that satisfies you and whatever happens after that is beyond your control. Sometimes you get recognition for it, sometimes you don't. Obviously the awards I've received are satisfying and they reinforce my self-belief, but at the same time I never forget that recognition can be quite an unpredictable, fleeting thing. So it's important to make sure you do the best you are capable of, because ultimately you have to satisfy yourself.

BALANCING COMMITMENT AND SELF-CARE

In healthy self-care we can find the freedom to choose and direct our own lives, and that is nurturing indeed.

The Women's Comfort Book, Jennifer Louden

As important as it is to commit to the dreams that inspire us, it is equally important to commit to taking good care of ourselves on the journey. Achievement is not just about external goals, it's about personal wellbeing. Our ability to bring our dreams into reality will be greatly enhanced by the sensitivity, support and nurturing we give to ourselves.

As we juggle our many roles, it's important to be aware of feelings of mental or physical tiredness, stress or overload and take steps to alleviate these. We may get away with neglecting our needs and pushing ourselves for a time but the cost to our health and quality of life is high if we continue to choose this path. We all need to take time out to enjoy the simple pleasures: to notice the change of seasons, gaze at the clouds in the blue sky, hear the birds sing or simply to feel the sun on our face.

For most of us it is an ongoing challenge to achieve a balance in our life. There is a tension between personal needs and responsibility to perform the many tasks required of us. External pressures compete for our time and energy and there is often little of either left for ourselves. As women we are socialised to place others' needs ahead of our own. We may feel uncomfortable or selfish if we attempt to prioritise our needs but in fact it is vital that we do. Continuing to give to others when we are depleted leads to resentment and exhaustion. When we care for ourselves first, we can then reach out to others from a position of strength and this is far more satisfactory for all. If we lead a busy life, developing the ability to say 'no' to other people's demands can be one of our most useful skills.

Self-care is about self-awareness, self-acceptance and gentleness. It's about noticing the physical, emotional, mental and spiritual signals that are telling us we are under stress, needing a break or hurting. It's about seeing ourselves as important and creating the time and space we need for rest, solitude, reflection, recreation, social activities and fun.

If we know we are becoming depleted, we can choose to acknowledge this and schedule some time to rest as soon as possible, or we can ignore our feelings and continue to push on relentlessly. The choices we habitually make reflect our commitment to ourselves and over time impact on our wellbeing.

It is vital to incorporate some form of self-care into our timetable on a daily basis. This may include regular trips to the gym, preparing healthy meals and all manner of lifestyle changes, but we need to beware of setting ourselves up for failure by overcommitting ourselves. These kind of strategies can take considerable energy and we can quickly become demoralised if we fail to meet self-care goals that are set unrealistically high. In fact self-care can consist of nurturing moments woven into our daily life: a few minutes sitting down with a cup of tea, a walk in the garden, using calming self-talk when we are stressed or leaving our telephone on answerphone when we are tired. We can also schedule, as a priority, regular time with family and friends, fun outings, massage, enjoyable physical activities and inspirational reading.

When we feel deprived and depleted, our capacity for achievement is limited. If we begin to notice that the harder we push ourselves the less we accomplish, we need to take this as a definite signal that we are becoming burnt out. We then need rest and extra self-care. We owe it to ourselves to be our own best support person, guardian and nurturer. We can't expect anyone else to meet our self-care needs for us. The questions on page 251 will enable you to access your level of self-care and develop a list of nurturing strategies.

The truth is, the more we support and care for ourselves, the more energy and personal power we will have to pursue our dreams. When we take time out to relax and enjoy ourselves, we become more productive. When we feel rested and replenished we are capable of achieving great things. Barbara Kendall and Sue Bradford are both passionate women with a huge commitment to their particular endeavours. Their stories reflect their awareness of the necessity of balancing commitment with consistent self-care.

Barbara Kendall

'If something bad happens then obviously I'm not quite on track and I need to do something differently.'

Barbara is one is our most successful, consistent and enduring sportswomen. She has put her heart and soul into her windsurfing for the past thirteen years. Her tremendous dedication to her sport has been rewarded by her numerous achievements, including winner of a gold medal in the Olympic Games at Barcelona in 1992, winner of a silver medal at the Atlanta Olympic games in 1996, winner of a bronze medal at the Sydney Olympic Games in 2000 and three times winner of the New Zealand Sportswoman of the Year award.

Barbara was born in Auckland in 1967 and grew up in a family of three children, all interested in sailing, and when she was 10 the whole family sailed to Fiji. Although her first love was dancing, Barbara began sailing P-class yachts competitively when she was 12 years old. After leaving school Barbara taught modern jazz for almost three years before fully pursuing her passion in windsurfing. Since the age of 19, she has been successfully competing all over the world. Now at 33 she is speaking of retirement. She wants to have some free time and fun, begin a family and perhaps return to her work as a dance teacher. But when questioned about the possibility of competing in the future, Barbara replies with a grin, 'Never say never!'

In the earlier years windsurfing was absolutely an obsession. It was all I wanted to do and it was just the most ultimate sport. I did it in competition and for a job and for holidays. It was a huge thing in my life because it was something that I loved so much.

Competing at the Olympic Games at Atlanta in 1996 was one of the biggest learning curves I've had. I was so nervous and coping with those nerves was tough. Learning from the mistakes I made and then really working on that for a couple of years was really important. It took me that time to get to grips with the psychological side of putting it right and then away I went. So in 1998 I ended up winning the World Championships by really concentrating on fixing the things I wasn't so good at back then.

One of the things I needed to learn was how to actually accept my nerves instead of trying to fight them. Realising that I actually had to have nerves because that's where we get our adrenaline from helped, learning to use them as a positive instead of a negative. Instead of dreading the fact that I'm going to go out to race, actually looking forward to it. Most of us go into competition and think, 'Oh no! What's going to be the outcome? Oh God!' Instead of saying, 'Oh cool! Let's go and see what happens.' So I focused on just wanting an above average day and that really helped.

Learning about the psychology of winning has been probably been one of the most interesting things for me over the last few years. Realising that every time you go into a competition you're a different person. You've got a different set of circumstances and a different set of people around you and you're in a different country. Just coping with all that well so you can still compete at your best is a challenge. When you get to the top level of the competition it's not, 'Who's the best athlete?' It's, 'Who's the best psychological athlete?' It's the brain! It's getting that in control so you can control your highs and your lows.

What I've learnt over the last few years is I need to try and get into the state I know I work the best in. I've got to be totally relaxed, I've got to be happy and excited and I've got to be energised. It's just making sure I've got those factors covered and I've got a positive outlook on what I'm doing. I try to never think in the negative because as soon as I doubt myself it tends to come back at me and things start going wrong. It's really important to learn from everything and just put out the positive and then hopefully the right things happen.

For the last four years my husband Shayne has travelled with me. It's made a big difference to have my buddy and soul mate with me the whole time. I've got someone to go through the highs and the lows with — someone to bounce ideas off, to fix my equipment, to cook for me, hang out with and to see the sights with. Shayne competes in races as well, so we're always discussing things. We balance each other out in personalities. Even though we're quite individualistic we just go together in our own little way. Shayne's quite laid-back and casual and his whole goal in life is just to be happy. I'm more determined and more into striving for things.

When I was travelling by myself in those early days it was really tough. I was the only New Zealander travelling with people from a whole lot of different countries. We were competing against each other but we'd be sharing cars, accommodation, equipment, just so we could actually make it. So you had to be friends with your arch rivals. I had to learn how to get on with people in a high stress situation. I ended up building a wall around myself so nothing affected me, hiding my emotions so I could cope with it all and I actually became very tough. I don't think it was a very healthy position to be in. Then I'd just come home and melt and spend hours talking to my mum about whether I was doing the right thing. She was amazing. Some days she'd just sense that I needed to talk and she wouldn't go to work that day. She's such a neat lady.

One of the main difficulties in the beginning was the fact that being in New Zealand we were so isolated from competition. The only way I was ever going to become good was to base myself overseas, so I ended up living in Hawaii for about seven or eight years. Obviously the financial side of it was a huge obstacle. For me to be able to do the Olympic circuit I had to earn money in the professional circuit to fund my Olympic campaign because there was no prize money in the Olympics and I didn't have that many sponsors to fund it. I was always on the hell budget compared to everybody else. I think the government gave me $4000 for 1992 for a whole Olympic campaign for a year.

In the beginning I put so much pressure on myself to do well, to earn the prize money so I could go to the next event, because if I didn't succeed in a competition I didn't make it to the next one and that would be it. After the Olympics in 1992 it was a little bit easier to get sponsors because I won the gold medal. Probably one of the reasons I've been so successful in the last few years has been the sponsorship I now have. Since 1996 I've just concentrated purely on Olympic class racing. Without financial worries I've been able to do exactly what I wanted to do.

I had a really tough four years from 1987 right through to about 1991. There were injuries as well, from accidents — broken wrists and stitches. I was overseas in Hawaii and I had to look after myself. In the space of two years I had about five or six accidents that put me in hospital and put me out for three or four weeks. With the last one, I just about cut my arm off and was told I'd never windsurf again. That made me stop and think. I realised my head wasn't connected to my body and I wasn't thinking about what I was doing. I was charging on too much. I needed to slow down. I think I've been learning that lesson the whole time. Like in 1997 I was sick just about all year with fatigue, just pushing myself too hard. It wasn't until I just about fell off the cliff that I went, 'Hold on I'm not doing something quite right here. I keep getting sick over and over and I don't have any energy. What's going on?'

Self-care is a huge factor. I've learned as soon as I have an injury or illness or any sort of niggle, I need to start doing something about it straightaway because I've only got one body and how I feel about myself affects how I approach everything I do. If I'm confident about my body and my health then I'm going to be good. I know if I haven't got the energy then I need to start asking myself: 'Why am I feeling tired? Is it a diet thing? Is it sleep deprivation thing? Is it a deficiency in my vitamins or minerals? Is it a niggling injury? Is it my thought processes?' Then I need to work to get myself back on track. That's really important in our game because it really is a mind-game.

Alternative medicine has been a big factor in my wellbeing over the last few years. I've looked into homeopathic medicine and have done a bit of Alexander Technique and a lot of cranial osteopathy. I'm seeing a guy at the moment who removes all the toxins from your body and I've noticed a huge difference with that. Also I work closely with a masseuse, Janice McLennan, who does very special energy power healings.

Meeting Janice has probably changed my life because it's really opened up the spiritual dimension for me and that's been fascinating. With the lessons she's taught me about myself and my body and competing and stress, I've become more in tune with myself. Since I first worked with her in 1995 I've learned about opening my soul and visualisation and watching what happens to my body when I meet somebody. Learning to breathe properly from my diaphragm has also been a big one. She's been actually a big factor in a lot of my success over the last couple years.

When I'm feeling a bit down or tired I practise visualisation by consciously going to a mental space where I feel really contented, like imagining myself walking along a surf beach or sailing in a yacht with the water all sparkling. That's a way of bringing my energy up again because that feeds my soul.

I do get burnt-out at times but I believe that's what happens if we put a lot of energy into something that's important. Like any dance production, any exam or anything you work towards, you're really mentally tired from it when it's finished. I think that's normal and if we're not burnt-out after doing something big then obviously we didn't put everything we had into it.

After the Olympics if you don't experience burnout then you haven't done it right. The American have named it post-Olympic depression. It can last quite a while until you start sorting out what you want to do. I had it for about five months after Barcelona. I didn't want to windsurf. I was retiring. That was it! So I did other things and caught up on life and then I thought, 'I actually really enjoy this sport,' and away I went again. I know from experience that I need to give myself time to recover and start to get that hunger back again when I feel like that. Being older and a lot more experienced I do recognise that more now. When I was younger I tended to just charge on and become exhausted.

I've always been really fortunate because I've had an amazing network of support underneath me, my mum and dad and Shayne and my coach and Janice and my sister and brother and my friends. The important thing has been just knowing that no matter what I achieve I'm always going to be me and that's what people like. Mum and Dad always encouraged us to have goals and they've never put limitations on us. They never said, 'You can't do that.' When my grandparents were alive they were the same sort of amazing people. My Nana died at 85 but she still seemed like a 30-year-old. She was always young, always into things and she never said no. It was like, 'Nana, do you want to go to the pictures?' and she'd always say, 'Yes!' I believe that's what keeps you going and going.

I've really enjoyed what I've done. I like excitement of it. It's been such amazing learning but I'm ready for a change. I've had eight months of the year travelling for the last fifteen years. In the beginning it was fun but for the last five years it's actually been pretty tough. All our friends are having kids and settling down and moving on with life and here we are still skittering around the world. We've had an unfinished house for the last three years. I can't do the things I want to do because I know the dedication it takes to be the best. So I miss out on my sister's kids growing up, having birthdays, friends' weddings and things like that. That's been the biggest sacrifice.

It's a good feeling though, to feel that I've done exactly what I wanted to do and learnt as much as I possibly could. I feel like I've just about exhausted all possibilities. And I've changed. For me it used to be, 'Oh wow, it's windy, got to go sailing', and now it's more like, 'Oh I don't really want to get wet.' I don't feel regret about that. I feel I've fulfilled that whole need now. In the future I'll probably go windsurfing for fun every now and then, but it'll be really frustrating to know how I used to be and not be able to push the limits as much.

I've had an amazing life so far because I've known what I wanted to do and I've loved doing it. I could say that I'm lucky, but really it's been more about knowing what I want and going out and getting it. I always have this vision of what I'd like to achieve and that's what I go for.

I don't have a religion but I believe in karma and if you're a good person what more can you do? You do good, you do your part for society and help and that's what it's all about. I believe that if you put the right things out there you get what you're after. I believe that everything always happens for a reason. If something bad happens then obviously I'm not quite on track and I need to do something differently. I'm definitely into that.

I think that every day is a miracle. There's so many funny things that happen, and so many awesome things that we can take for granted. We can tend to get so wound up in what we're doing that we don't notice all the little intricacies of life. Like little baby quails being born and skipping up onto the terrace or an amazing sunset or a flower that just came out or when it pours down with rain or a really windy day. How often do we put our car radio on full bore and sing at the top of our lungs? I listen to Mikey Havoc in the morning on BFM for two hours when he's on. Sometimes I'm in my car driving and listening to him and I'm just laughing my head off. That's what it's about. Good laughs!

I think those are the things that are really important. Once you stop noticing all those little funny things and all those really neat things in life then why are you here? We've just got to keep reminding ourselves to keep looking out for them. Remembering to stop and think, 'Hold on a minute. That's a really cool sunset.' Becoming more consciously aware of those things that we can take for granted. I practise that all the time.

Barbara's message

Maybe I'm a dreamer but I believe if you really want to do something then you should just go for it, because if your heart and soul and energy is into it then you're going to be successful. If you keep looking back over your shoulder and thinking, 'Oh gosh, I should have done that', then you'll regret it because you're not living to your potential.

A lot of people get lost and don't know exactly what they want to do. They go off one way because that's what expected of them: 'You've got to get a job, you've got to get money . . .' instead of saying, 'Hold on. This is what I really want to do.' How much money do you need to earn to live off? You don't actually need that much if you're doing what you love. I believe if you really want to do something there must be a way of being able to survive and keep doing it.

The parents of one of my friends wanted to kayak around the coast of Turkey and at the age of 60 they're doing it. They built this special kayak and off they went and that's so inspirational. There are unlimited possibilities if you really want to do something. Who cares whether it's kayaking around Turkey or going to a cooking class? If that's what you want to do then I think you should just go for it. When you keep flexible in your thinking that's what keeps you young. Start making the plans because it will happen if you really want to do it.

Sue Bradford

'. . . until everyone has a chance to be fulfilled in this world I cannot be complete either.'

Sue is renowned for her passionate concern for the disadvantaged in our society, having worked for many years at the grassroots level to raise people's awareness about the plight of the unemployed. Despite considerable personal hardship and sacrifice and being arrested many times for her involvement in demonstrations, Sue has remained true to her cause.

After studying for an MA in History, Sue completed a one-year post graduate course in journalism in 1974. In 1976 Sue gave birth to twins and spent what she describes as three depressing years on the DPB. During this time she went back to University to study Chinese and graduated with first class honours. Since marrying Bill in 1980, Sue has given birth to three more children. One of her twin sons suffered from schizophrenia and died tragically in 1995.

Sue was involved in the setting up of the Unemployed Workers' Rights Centre in 1983 and in 1990 helped to establish the People's Centre, a community self-help organisation which provides inexpensive services and advocacy to people in need. Over the years Sue coordinated these organisations, often working for little or no wage. She also tutored part time at Unitec in the Diploma in Not for Profit Management. Sue is now a Green Party Member of Parliament. She lives in Wellsford with her family on a farm they run in a cooperative way with a priest and nun.

I've always felt strongly about poverty and injustice. I grew up that way and it's affected my life. As long as I can remember I've been upset about things that I saw as not good in the world. When I was quite young I was really conscious that some people had OK lives, and I was one of them, but other people didn't and I had a choice about which side I was on.

I first got involved in political groups when I was 13 and at school in America. The Vietnam War was on and we were in Madison, the home of one of the ten biggest air force bases in America. They used to have nuclear air-raid signs outside the school and air-raid shelters in the basement so I was very conscious of the threat of nuclear war. Those were big issues for me – fear of the world going up in nuclear warfare and seeing the Vietnam War killing people. When I was 15 I made a conscious choice that I'd put my life on the side of the people who didn't have much, so that when I died I could feel that at least I'd tried to do something to make things better.

For most of my adult life now I've been working in Unemployed Workers' groups. I guess one thing I've learnt through that is tenacity. Trying to make any real change to people's lives or society is a long haul. My personal motivation for being in the unemployed and beneficiaries' movement is that I hate unemployment. As a group we were often labelled as dole bludgers or useless beneficiary scum. That kind of attitude towards us was upsetting. Just to be treated as though we were worth nothing, year after year, no matter what we did and no matter what we had to offer, really hurt when the only reason most of us were working in our group was to end unemployment. A lot of our time went into looking at solutions to unemployment. Time after time we tried to tell politicians there were some ways forward, but nobody wanted to listen to us. That's really what led me to get into Parliament. I knew I had to try to get that message through at another level.

There have been tough times, like when my husband Bill and I were both sent to jail totally out of the blue on the same day after a demonstration and we still had lots of kids at home. Times like that you get pretty angry and desperate. But we kept going. When you know the powerlessness of being locked in a cell your whole world changes. I've been in Mount Eden Prison twice, only for short periods, but they were quite profound – going from running a big organisation and a big family to being nothing. It's very humiliating. It was really shocking to me to know what it was like to be a prisoner and have society and the state turned against me in that way. It made me really think and reaffirm whose side I was on, because there are people a lot more powerless than me.

And yet I found it quite a deep experience. The solidarity of the women and some of the conversations I had with them were really mind blowing. I knew if I ever ended up in jail for a longer period I'd turn that into good because I'd learn so much – even though it's really awful and I'd never like to go there again. That's how I survive – by looking at what good I can get out of the situation, by looking for the good in everyone and by looking for the common ground in political work.

I've learned how to roll with the punches, how to be knocked over or hurt by political or personal situations and keep going any-way. It is hard but you don't just give up and go home. What helps me in those situations is support from the people round me. I've got a very strong relationship with Bill. We've been together for over twenty years and we're a very close family. And I've always had strong per-sonal support groups, as well as political ones.

The sort of work I've done with people who are having a hard time has taught me to be truly humble, to know that any of us can be in a state of madness or a state or despair. It can happen to anyone. I've had rough times in my life where I've been very low, depressed like heaps of other people are, but I've been able to come through those. I always tautoko or acknowledge anyone who's been through those experiences. It's so hard. Sometimes I feel that I'm still recov-ering from being absolutely at rock bottom where I've just had nothing left. So I'm conscious of that in other people. I acknowledge other people's difficulties and the worth of their personal struggles. Going through the fire and coming out the other side and rebuilding your life is a really good thing to do.

I've been through total depression in several situations when I was younger and I'll never forget what that space is like and that in itself is really valuable. I would never say that will never happen to me again. Something could go wrong in my life. I could lose my partner or some-thing of myself. I was in the process of recovery from depression for a long time and I got out by going step by step. Finding activities outside myself and having children was a big part of it. Also I went back to university part time and that gave me something to do that I really enjoyed. I also met Bill and we had a good relationship and that helped. Mine is a pretty classic story really.

The worst thing that ever happened to me was losing my oldest son, one of my twins. It's over five years now but I can just flip back into it like it was yesterday. I'm still totally devastated. I don't know how you get over it. In a way I don't think you ever do. All you can do is survive and try to keep it in balance and perspective. But that doesn't always happen. Losing a child by any means is terrible, but by suicide is a really bad way. I certainly care a lot about the mental health system now.

At the time it happened I spoke out because I wanted to turn my anger into something useful but it's pretty weird being up there in the media when you're going through something like that. Afterwards lots of people really wanted me to keep active in the mental health area. I made a very conscious decision not to because I could see it would suck my whole life out. Instead I continued to do the work that I was doing with unemployed people and beneficiaries.

Now that I'm a Member of Parliament I've reversed my decision and decided to pick up mental health as well. Even if I can do a little bit to help people through my position it's something. So I'm speaking out now and trying to push the government along a bit. There's so many people who have lost people because of mental illness and there are lots of people now still having a terrible time. Anything I can do to make that better is worthwhile. I feel I owe it to my son and to my family and to everyone else who suffers to try to do something about mental health.

I learnt long ago how important fitness is as a way for me to get a bit of distance from things. Sometimes it's been the only way that I've physically and mentally survived. It's so inbuilt now I just do it. I do slow jogging, nothing more sophisticated than that. I love swimming as well. I try to eat well and healthily and be quite disciplined. I need to be because I work really long hours. For a lot of my life I've had to be very disciplined about time for myself, time for the kids, time for fitness, time for work. Going to Parliament was just another step. Even before I did this I was commuting from Wellsford to Auckland for work on a daily basis for five years and that was very exhausting.

I recharge myself by having time with my family. I've always structured in a good break every summer to go away camping in the north by the sea, going back to basics — living under the trees, cooking over the open fire. That's a big nourishment to my body and soul. And I read a lot. Reading is an absolutely necessary part of my life I can't do without. It gives me great joy to read good books, entering into other people's lives and thinking about other things. I love movies too, for the same reason. The work I do now is really intense so it's good to get some space from it, whether it's through some sort of meditation or reading or exercise.

As the years have gone by I've had a lot to do with religious people, including a lot of sisters and brothers of the Catholic Church and I've enjoyed the experience of mixing with those people. I'm very interested in theology and I continue to develop some consciousness, but I'm not attached to any faith or cult or religion. I do believe that until everyone has a chance to be fulfilled in this world I cannot be complete either. I think having compassion and love and trying to change the world so everyone has a chance is a spiritual thing to do. That's been at the core of my value system since I was a kid.

I do try to consciously step back and listen to what some people would call God, to hear what's really going on and to let that voice come through. If there's a big problem or I don't know what to do I try to just let it sit for a bit until something clear comes through to me and usually it does. I've consciously used that method for about twenty-five years and the more I use it the more it works. I'm not saying that it always works or that I use it enough, but I do try to let that voice come to me.

I've always been open to change or to changing my mind on something or viewing things from another point of view and yet I really try to hold true to my core beliefs. I'm really into Taoist and early Chinese Buddhist philosophy, which to me is all about being clear and flexible, but staying strong inside that and listening to the inner voice. Within that it's important to be able to hear the different points of view or if a situation has changed to be flexible and not be afraid of change. I believe even quite radical change, even in one's own life, is often a good thing, though at first it's hard.

Like in 1999, just before I went into Parliament, I lost my base group and my job. That was all really difficult stuff to deal with, but I needed to acknowledge that I was working through a time of change. I didn't know what was going to happen. Maybe I was going to go to Parliament, but maybe I was going to be unemployed. I had six months like that. Now I feel that the risk was worth it. I did know that if it all turned to shit and I didn't get to Parliament, which was just as likely as anything else, that there were other options. I might end up registering at WINZ but I'd also be trying to get jobs or wanting to take some other path in my life that might lead to other wonderful things. I was open to whatever was going to happen. I'm a risk taker, but to make change you need to be. As long as there's life there's hope really, clichéd though that sounds. I think you can only work in the way I do if you've got hope for the future or you wouldn't bother. You have to hope that things will be better for our children.

In my new role as an MP the hardest thing is being away from home so much when one of my kids is still under 11, even though his dad is there and it's a good situation. I've never abandoned my family to this extent before. I find it tearing and sad to be away from all of them, but my son particularly because he's still so young. I've always been conscious about avoiding sacrificing myself or the people close to me for my work. I believe to be any good at changing the world you have to put yourself and your children first. Because if you go under yourself or if you let your kids down, there's no point in doing anything else.

I sometimes wish I'd gone to Parliament ten years ago when I was physically and mentally stronger and younger. Dealing with tiredness and exhaustion is a challenge. Yet I'm glad I've had that ten years because I've learnt so much with working in the People's Centre and all the other community work I've done. I've come to realise that it's actually better to be bringing experience than youth to Parliament, so I don't regret it.

One of the things I'm not good at even now is saying 'no' to people who want things from me. I've come to realise I need to protect myself more with this job. The demands on you are so huge that you could give every minute of twenty-four hours a day, every day of the year, and it would still be a drop in a bucket compared to what people want. It was a bit like that for me before but it's really intensified. I'm so used to being open to people and open to invitations, shutting myself off is quite hard.

One of the main things that has kept me going, especially over the last ten years since I became more of a public figure, has been ordinary people saying encouraging things to me in the supermarket or in the street or on the phone or a letter. Ordinary beneficiaries or mothers – people who aren't in the public eye – who say something like, 'You're fighting for me. I'd never have the courage to come on a demo. I'd never be able to go to Parliament.' I've had an enormous amount of that kind of support and it's fantastic. Those people have been a huge part of what's kept me going. I can never thank them enough. It's really made me realise the people know what we're trying to do and they're behind us and that's all that matters.

Sue's message

Try to find your heart's desire or where your passion lies and follow that. If you're not sure, talk to people who can help you work out what you really want to do in your life. For me, when I was younger with the twins and very depressed, it was learning the Chinese language. That wasn't necessarily going to take me anywhere – well it did take me to China – but it was something that I really, passionately wanted to do. It could be joining a community group or a political party or becoming a volunteer. It's finding something outside yourself that you feel strongly about and you're able to do.

I believe if you're in a bad situation you can build out of it step by step. I can only speak from my own experience but for me it was important to break out of the four walls of my home. If you've got children it's not that they're not important but it's that you need something else that's important as well, so it's good to build relationships with friends and partners outside that. Find people to work with in whatever thing you want to do. Undoubtedly believing in something outside of yourself is helpful, even if that's just believing in the power of the love of other people.

LISTENING TO
INNER WISDOM

We all begin with the question 'What am I, really? What is my work here?'

Women Who Run With the Wolves, Clarissa Pinkola Estés

Our inner wisdom is a rich source of the inspiration from which dreams are created. Many of our best ideas come when we take the time to relax and reflect, become aware of our insights, consider options and tap into deeper wisdom. Each of us has an inner knowing which guides us towards harmony and health. It signals when something is not right for us and guides us in finding creative answers to the questions that trouble us. Our ability to recognise these signals depends on our awareness of our inner world.

Our busy lives demand much attention. We can get so caught up in processing the necessary information, fact-finding, organising, strategising and racing against the clock, we overlook our need for time to focus within. Amid our busyness we endeavour to bring our intellect to bear on problems and our tired mind wrestles with them hoping to find a solution, but often this approach does not give us the best results. Too much effort can become counterproductive because it interferes with our creativity and wisdom. When we find it most difficult to slow our thoughts and activity we usually need to find a way to create some quiet time.

Taking time for regular self-reflection can make a huge difference to our wellbeing. It's in the quietness and stillness within that we will find fresh perspectives, deeper knowledge, new clarity and renewed energy and creativity. When we quieten the chatter of our thinking we move from worrying to discovering new insights and solutions that were there all the time but obscured by all our activity.

Quiet reflection times allow us to stay connected to who we really are and help us to bring balance into our lives. If we are to pursue our interests decisively and confidently it is vital we maintain a link between the various roles we play and our true feelings, needs and desires; our outer and inner worlds. It's important to regularly take time out of our busy schedules to attend to our feelings, check we feel on track in our life, notice our emotional responses to various situations and people and become aware of any feelings of disquiet. We are able to move forward most powerfully when we have acknowledged and met our emotional, mental, physical and spiritual needs. Taking reflection time will help us to see how to correct any imbalances in our lives. Ces Lashlie is a woman who is fully aware of the personal power that is generated from the self-knowledge and self-acceptance gained from personal reflection.

Ces Lashlie

'I believe that at almost every point there are choices. Life is about laying yourself open to the choices and being prepared to take the risks.'

Ces is well known for her passion in the area of social justice and commitment to breaking down the barriers between prison inmates and the community. Ces was married at 19 and separated seven years later with two children aged 2 and 4 years old. She then returned to Victoria University to complete her BA in Anthropology and Maori. In 1984 she began work as a Probation Officer and eighteen months later became the first woman prison officer to work in a male prison, starting in Wi Tako Prison in Wellington. As other women followed Ces into male prisons it became apparent that the biggest challenge came not from the inmates but from the women's fellow officers. The men were uncomfortable with the reality that women could do the job and were not slow in showing their disapproval and disdain. In an attempt to ease the situation for the women, the position of Penal Division Equal Opportunities Coordinator was created and Ces was appointed in March 1990. As part of her job Ces conducted seminars with 1800 prison officers throughout the various prisons in New Zealand, working to challenge the macho attitudes and behaviour that remained so prevalent. Gradually her blend of straight talking and clarification of the issues contributed to positive changes in the prison culture.

After spending some time as a Prison Inspector, Ces became the manager of the Christchurch Women's Prison in 1997. She was a driving force behind the two Christchurch Arts Festival productions held at the prison in 1997 and 1999, in which the inmates told their life stories in harrowing detail through music and drama. These powerful performances gave thousands of people insight into the reality behind an inmate's journey to prison. Ces left her position at the Christchurch Women's Prison in September 1999. She is currently working as a management/ social justice consultant.

I live life with passion. My greatest aim is to live with deep intimacy every day of my life. I'm the mother of two adult children I raised on my own. I think a lot of my journeying has been framed by parenthood, by having to raise these children by myself, and my sense of what I wanted them to be equipped with in terms of the world. I've learned a great deal from that. Being a mother is incredibly important to me. Even in my worst moments when I ask, 'Have I made a difference? Is my life worth anything?' I can turn and look at my two children and I know that whatever else life is about, I've actually got this living proof that I have contributed something to the world.

I've always had a strong sense of social justice which has come from my childhood. My father was an alcoholic and there's no doubt that has been a driving force behind what I've done. He was a very intelligent man but he had his own ghosts to deal with as a result of the war. So I have a strong interest in what lies behind problems. What leads people down certain paths? I was very conscious of the tormented part of my father's soul I guess and it's led me on through a variety of steps to think about social justice — to think about the degree to which people are disconnected from their soul and therefore the chaos in which they live.

I think my childhood gave me a sense that all was not as it seemed. My adult experience has shown me that is often the case. In our family there was always a sense of two agendas running. On the surface I was from a middle-class Catholic family, yet I was aware of the secret themes running under my life and so became aware of the themes running under other people's lives. My childhood taught me not to move in and judge too fast on appearances.

A large part of my finding my way to adulthood was about suppressing my intuition and trying to operate without it. This latter part of my adulthood has been the journey of fully integrating intuition back into my life so that now I'm at the point where I'm incredibly comfortable with it. I'm drawn to the exploration of what life is about and the journey each of us is on — going deeper and deeper into that concept of self-actualisation and finding full inspiration with yourself.

But social justice is the theme that runs through pretty much everything I get involved with.

My focus is largely about bringing intuition and people's souls into the workplace. If we're really going to make a difference to the culture we've got to get back to intuition – to the soul part of people. It's not enough to apply analytical, logical business practice. But using intuition can make us vulnerable because we have no tangible proof of what it is we're suggesting should happen. To many people if they can't touch it and feel it, it doesn't exist. My argument is that's an absolute nonsense.

I am a reasonably spiritual person in the sense of the connectedness between people. It's been absolutely essential that I learn to know myself well and I spend a great deal of time mapping my inner as well as my outer journey. For me writing in a journal has been an important part of my self-awareness because it allows me to bring to a conscious level the things that are lingering on the corner of my consciousness. That's how I've become more in tune with myself. I'm naturally an introvert which people find really strange because I can stand up and talk and I project out so well. But every time I do something that puts me out there I have to have the equivalent period alone in order to replenish myself.

Some of my understanding of myself has came from the book *Women Who Run With the Wolves* by Clarissa Pinkola Estés. That book has been a huge influence, almost like my Bible. I intrinsically believe in the beauty of women in the way that the book describes. I love her idea that women aren't these soft, careful creatures. In their natural form women are wild like wolves. They're out there, and their beauty comes from that strength.

For a lot of my working life in the prison service I needed to consciously put on an armour in order to be able to achieve what I wanted to do. That armour allowed me to go in and develop the techniques to meet the prison service at the forefront. I was the first woman to work in a male prison as an officer and that was always going to be dangerous – not physically dangerous, but spiritually dangerous!

I was able to meet belligerent prison officers on their own ground and really take them on at their own level. Although I can do that very easily, I know that in doing it I'm wearing armour against the male bureaucracy of the organisation. I've developed a reputation for being quite hard-nosed. I can put on the tough macho role if I want to, but it's like adopting a persona. It's been essential that I've learned that because otherwise there's a danger of being swept up in the role. There have been moments of self-examination when I asked myself if I'd become this person. Now I know myself well enough to know that role isn't me. Even so eventually I knew I had to step back from it because there was a cost.

I am a frontier person. I've been the one who operated at the edge and pushed things just that much further. There's been a desolation and a loneliness attached to that, when for whatever reason it's suddenly appeared as if I'm working alone. Because I've been physically surrounded by a lot of men, I've forgotten there are a circle of women friends, standing just behind me and in many cases around me to support me. That's hugely important to me.

My decision to leave Christchurch Women's Prison was about knowing that I had become incredibly disconnected from my soul. I was being woven more and more into the work and it was killing me. Plus I'd achieved some of the larger aims that I'd intended. Three months before I left I remember ringing a friend and saying, 'I don't think I'm going to make it.' It wasn't any dramatic physical thing, it was that I'd become so disconnected I felt like I was operating outside myself. I was thinking, 'How did I get to this stage? What is it that I've neglected that suddenly I have this feeling of disconnection from my life purpose, from the meaningfulness of what I've been doing?' I'd always been so focused about that and suddenly I wasn't.

I realised in order to manage in that environment I had begun to put parts of myself away and I'd also done that as a mother and as manager as well. I was aware that there was a whole part of my life sitting in a box – this box of me – of me the person, of Celia, rather than Ces the prison person or Cecelia the manager. Whole parts of me had been neglected while I'd raised my children and established a profile and made a difference career-wise.

When I resigned from Christchurch Women's it was a huge decision to change direction like that. What I was literally doing was saying to fate, or the gods or goddesses, 'Here, you show me what's next. I'm not going to plan it like I always do. I'm going to let fate take it.' That was a challenge! It's one thing to ask the questions but it's another to find out if you're attuned enough to know if the answer is sitting in front of you. It was trusting enough to say, 'OK, I'm not sure what the next step is but I feel I should be looking to take a different approach and to free myself up.'

When I left the prison there was this enormous accolade. They dedicated a farewell performance of the show we'd been doing to me and people flew from all over New Zealand to be there. All these lovely things were said. It was like being at your own funeral. Suddenly I was a hero. Even the bosses actually affirmed what a good image I'd put forward as a manager of a public prison.

Then within months there was a fairly fundamental issue I was involved in and suddenly I was crucified again as the one who was wrong. It was a big moment of desolation until I talked to people who refocused it for me. There was this question of, 'How did I move from hero to villain in six months? Why do I always go that extra mile and suddenly find myself wrong again? Am I never happy with what I've done?' And the biggest question of all was, 'Do I do it to myself?' It was important to think about what this was telling me about me.

After I resigned I was asked to apply for a job managing a women's prison in Brisbane. The practical part of me said, 'That's a good thing to do. It would be firm employment. It would be interesting,' but by the time they were ready I'd found my own place to live in Wellington and suddenly it was like my psyche was saying, 'This is a moment in your life where you should stop and not take the career decision. Make the soul decision.'

Finding my new house was interesting. Thirty seconds after I walked in the door I knew it was where I wanted to live. We signed the lease straightaway and as I walked down the pathway this voice in my head said, 'You don't have to go to Brisbane.' It was a relief because this is home, being among the network of people who have known me for a long time and being near my children. I could have done that job well and gained some further international exposure as a manager of women's prisons, but I had the absolutely tangible feeling that in coming home from Christchurch Women's I'd unpacked my soul. I had let it out. I'd begun to unpack the box of the parts of me and Brisbane would have required me to put them back in the box because I'd be going to the harsh Australian culture. It wasn't home. I'd be alone again and operating in the persona of a prison manager.

So I've stepped away from managing prisons because the armour gets very hard to carry and I do get weighed down by it. The next page in my life is to see what it's like to not have to wear the armour. I want to be so in touch with the core of my being that it gives me an inner protection; my sense of self and the boundaries of myself are so strong that people can come quite close and it's OK. I'm confident enough in myself to be able to walk away if I want to or to not do what they want. I don't need to protect myself by having them hit metal.

It's time to have some fun. It's time to not have to spend every moment of every day saving the world, which is what women can get desperately pulled into. I've spent a great deal of my life saving the world, first by raising two children the absolute best I could and then through the social justice issues. Now I'm giving myself permission not to do that. Which in the end will make me more effective in making a difference anyway.

It's also about welcoming abundance into my life and that can be very scary: I wouldn't want to have too much money or be too happy because life could take it away again. So now this is a tangible decision to say, 'Actually I'm welcoming in as much abundance as there is. I expect my life to be fantastic. I expect to have heaps of money, heaps of happiness and to always have really good work.' I've visualised it, now I just actually have to let it in. These last few months have been largely about finding my feet and accepting that it's OK to live this way.

It doesn't mean that I won't be out there, it just means that I will do it slightly less confrontationally and be less frightened that in so doing people might rob something from me, which is what I think my preoccupation was. I was afraid that they were going to take part of me away. I still feel very strongly about social justice. I'm very much for personal responsibility but within that there has to be a connectedness, an understanding of people's journeys and what leads them into prison so that we can help them make the decision not to go back again.

My thing is to cherish the difference between the genders. To allow for it and create a space in which you can enjoy it. So too with Pakeha and Maori. I'm heavily committed to tikanga Maori. I believe we are all diverse human beings and that there's so much more that can be gained if we work together. We all have strengths and weaknesses. It's that old thing of maximising the strengths and minimising the differences so that it becomes a workable environment.

It's not about climbing the fence and going in and weeding someone else's garden, thinking she should leave that relationship, or whatever. If I deal with my own garden I'm actually giving others the permission to do theirs and that's the greatest gift I can give them. To let them live their lives the way they want to and to have me interact with their lives to the degree they want.

In the aftermath of finishing in the prison service I have worked particularly hard to reconnect with myself and to keep my inner and outer journey interlinked. I've done that by taking the time. I'm lucky that I've landed some temporary work which has meant that I'm financially OK, so this has allowed me the space to focus on my inner journey. Even though my future employment prospects are not clear I'm not unduly worried because I trust this process.

Now in my mid-forties I'm much more aware of the rhythms of life and much more patient when I have the sense that something's going to come but this is not the right time. There is a rhythm and a reason for most things that happen. I believe that at almost every point there are choices. Life is about laying yourself open to the choices and being prepared to take the risks. I enjoy that comfort of knowing I am who I am. I believe it's only in giving yourself the space to be who you are that you can give other people the space to be who they are – and the magic comes from that.

Ces' message

Dare to make intuition part of your decision-making process day to day in the workplace. The challenge is how to use it and survive out in the corporate world we live in. I think of intuition as a muscle – if it isn't used it grows thin and wastes away. It's not something that sits there forever useable, you have to practise it. Writing is great for developing your intuition but it needs to be in a journal no one else is going to see, because often what we write appears to the world to be fanciful stuff. If you've got something you're dealing with, the musings of your journal can help you to put the pieces together. If you let yourself write non-judgmentally often the answers will come to you. It's an amazing process, so trust it!

Take the time to keep working on making a deep connection with yourself. And if you have left parts of you behind at crucial moments of your life have the courage to turn back and get them. I believe we get our power through our connection with ourselves, not through external things. Having that inner connection is so empowering.

SPEAKING OUT

Communication is power. Those who have mastered its effective use can change their experience of the world and the world's experience of them.

Unlimited Power, Anthony Robbins

Speaking our truth with conviction, gentleness and sensitivity is one of the most empowering actions we can take. Our ability to communicate effectively and stand up for what we want and believe could well be one of the deciding factors of our success. We are required to speak out if we are to influence others, engage their support and make the things we desire happen. The more self-awareness, self-esteem and sensitivity we have, the greater our ability to influence people in positive ways.

Our power to relate to people well is a measure of the respect, appreciation, acceptance and compassion we hold for them. Most high achievers have a positive attitude towards others and well-developed interpersonal skills. They are genuinely interested in people and demonstrate this by their warmth, courtesy and small but important gestures, such as remembering the other person's name and asking them questions about themselves.

Communication difficulties often arise when we perceive ourselves as either superior or inferior to another. Focusing on the differences in skills, status, wealth and culture widens the gulf between us, while remembering our shared humanity draws us closer together. We bridge differences when we treat others as our equal and relate freely from the heart as one human being to another.

The way we use our power has a profound impact on our relationships and the type of influence we have over people. We can use our power to uplift others by offering support and guidance. When we appreciate other's efforts, encourage them in their endeavours and let them know we believe in their potential, we help raise their confidence and empower them to achieve great things. We can also choose to use our power to undermine others by putting them down, overriding their opinions and needs and insisting on having our own way regardless of what they want.

Many people find handling conflict a challenge and will go to great lengths to avoid being put in a situation where they have to address difficult issues directly. However, despite our apprehension, when we have the courage to speak our truth, it often has a good outcome. When the real issues are honestly disclosed they can then be openly addressed. If we stay silent and passive when we have something important to say or reluctantly concede to other people's demands while hiding our dissatisfaction behind a false smile, we compromise ourselves and give our power away.

Some people try to deal with conflict by becoming insistent or forceful. While these tactics often get them what they want in the short term they also undermine others' goodwill and trust. Sometimes we come up against people who are determined to gain the upper hand at all costs. If this is an ongoing pattern of behaviour, very soon we are likely to find ourselves losing confidence and becoming increasingly distressed. It is then we need to protect ourselves by disengaging, gaining support and/or seeking the help of a counsellor to clarify how to deal effectively with this. Above all else we have the right to be treated with respect and it's vital we don't lose sight of this.

We ourselves may also become overbearing or destructive at times, heaping recriminations on someone or attacking their character. If we feel that person has upset or hurt us we may blame them for causing the difficulties but we are responsible for the way we choose to behave. As tempting as it may sometimes be to resort to hurtful behaviour, when we bring down the other person we also bring ourselves down as well. It is important to have our say on issues that concern us, but there is no honour in becoming aggressive and harsh. When we leave the other person with their dignity, we have also retained our own.

The best way to tackle a difficult situation is from a position of personal power. This is the stance of clarity, honesty and directness tempered with restraint. Personal power is about asserting our rights in a respectful manner; speaking our truth but not with the intention of doing harm to the other. This requires self-awareness, courage and integrity.

Assertive communication is something that many people struggle with but it's a skill which can be learned. There are many good books and courses available on the subject. The deceptively simple assertiveness techniques really can help to provide us with the tools to make our opinions known and stand our ground effectively if this is an area we find difficult. It can feel uncomfortable to be direct if we are not used to it but it does get easier with practice.

When we know ourselves well, are clear about our principles, values, rights and boundaries and have a respectful attitude towards others we are likely to use our power well. Merepeka Raukawa-Tait and Sukhi Turner are two women who have had the courage to speak out strongly on issues that were important to them and have held their ground despite considerable opposition.

Merepeka Raukawa-Tait

You want to be remembered for the message of hope or encouragement or support you gave . . .

Merepeka is the CEO of the National Collective of Independent Women's Refuges Inc. Known and admired for her powerful stand against domestic violence, Merepeka has come up against those who would silence her but has continued to speak out courageously. Having experienced domestic violence at first hand as a child, this is an issue dear to her heart.

No doubt Merepeka's rich life experience has contributed to her strength of character and ability to speak out with such conviction. At 21, Merepeka married a man from Switzerland and spent the next ten years living there, where she worked for the Chamber of Commerce. When this marriage ended Merepeka returned to New Zealand. Her second marriage, to a man with four children, also ended in divorce after seven years. Since 1980 Merepeka has: run a number of small businesses; held ministerial appointments on the National Advisory Council and the Employment of Women and the Maori Lands Advisory Boards; served as a trustee on a number of farm and forestry trusts; worked for the State Services Commission and Internal Affairs; served on the Bay of Plenty Regional Council for three years and managed the Maori Arts and Crafts Institute in Rotorua. Merepeka has an MBA in International Business Management.

Merepeka is now happily married to Theo Tait, a man who stands beside her and offers support for her challenging work. She greatly appreciates his encouragement, humour and wisdom. They live on a small whanau-run farm just outside Rotorua. Merepeka commutes to Wellington each week for her job, a reflection of her huge commitment to the work.

I feel really passionate about what I do. That's the fuel that gets me up in the morning. I see passion as a burning desire to make things happen and to be part of something that's bigger than yourself. I love my work and that's not only about doing something I'm enjoying, it's about knowing I'm actually making a contribution. Through my work I have an opportunity to contribute to the quality of life of thousands of women and children. I'd love to leave my current position with people saying, 'My God she turned the women's refuge around. We might never have heard of women's refuge before, or have had a negative view of it, but not now.'

When I look at the statistics for domestic violence I feel sad because I know that for every statistic there's a woman and children suffering. I feel very strongly that we have to do something about that. At the moment we're merely touching the tip of the iceberg. I'm determined to shoot the message home about domestic violence. In New Zealand we have a high degree of tolerance towards abuse but lately there's been a real groundswell of concern. People are responding all around the country.

I've had a backlash from some people who have taken exception to the fact I'm speaking out. They feel uncomfortable about me putting negative Maori statistics out there. They see me as having a go at our own, but I will not pull my head in. What I'm saying to them is, 'This is something we have to own up to. If in fact the statistics are bad for Maori then we need to know that. Sweeping the problem under the carpet isn't going to address it.' I don't want anyone saying to me that there are reasons for abusing children, because there's no excuse at all. I know colonisation has been a contributing factor to the mindset of some Maori people and I know about poverty but there is still no excuse for abuse, and I'm not going to have anybody trying to wriggle out of it.

Having good leadership is so important. If the leadership is inspirational and sets the standard, with clear expectations of what you want from people, then I believe people will rise to the occasion. People have said to me, 'You're against Maori men,' and I say, 'No I'm not against Maori men, but I'm against poor leadership and we haven't had leadership that's been invigorating.' We need leadership that uplifts Maori people, which says, 'You're destined for the very best. It's your right to be alongside everyone else in this world making a contribution.'

I've had a lot of publicity about my work. I'm going up and down the country speaking because there's a window of opportunity to really hammer home my message. Wherever I go people stop me and it's very nice to be congratulated and told you're doing good work, but I find the interviews and requests for meetings quite distracting. I need to concentrate on my work, but there's just so much coming at me. I can't keep up with the letters, e-mails, phone calls and faxes coming into the office every day. It's absolutely wonderful and they're all so encouraging and very supportive but I'm getting a little bit tired of the attention. I'm becoming alarmingly aware of this heavy expectation. People are saying things like, 'New Zealand needs strong women like you. You're there for all New Zealanders, not just Maori.' Just lately it's made me want to run away and hide for a little while.

In this job I've had to publicly speak about my own background, which hasn't been easy. I grew up in a home where my father was physically and emotionally abusive. There were many times when I picked my mother up off the floor. Because I was raising the issue of the abuse of women and children people started to ask, 'Who the hell is Merepeka and why is she speaking out in such a forthright manner?' The questions were becoming quite personal and so I spoke to my mother and two sisters and I said, 'If it becomes necessary for me to share a little bit about what we experienced as children I'd like your permission to do that,' and they gave me that permission.

There has been a downside to speaking about my childhood. My uncle took exception to it and sent a letter to the newspaper to say that he never saw my father's violence. But of course everyone knows the abuse of women and children usually happens when there's nobody else around. As far as I'm concerned if my mother and sisters have no objection to the fact that I'm speaking out then it's not for anybody else to question and take exception to it.

I grew up in a small town, Feilding, in the Manawatu. My father always worked but he drank and of course when you drink that takes money away from the family, so my mother always had to work as well to provide for us. She was very strong and always wanted the best for us. She was a full-blooded Maori woman, but we were never allowed to think we were victims in any way, shape or form. She always said, 'You're as good as the next person.' Although we experienced and saw some nasty things my father did to my mother she always said, 'You can do anything,' so we just grew up accepting that whatever we wanted to do we'd have a go at it.

The three things my mother often said when we were growing up were, 'My girls are beautiful. My girls can do anything. You must think and speak for yourself.' So we've always done that. My two sisters and I do think we're beautiful because for the first sixteen years before we left home that's what we heard. I think she just wanted to make sure that when we became women we would be strong, independent and outspoken – that we would carve our own future and not be dependent on anybody.

My own experience has shown me that what we say to our young children can either propel them to great heights or can keep them basically in the ditch. I know there are people in this country who never hear a word of affirmation in their home. There are thousands growing up in homes who don't have that supportive message coming through to them and that's very sad.

I was always very proud to be seen with my mother. She used to say, 'Never be afraid to stand out in a crowd.' Even if she wore the same outfit year in and year out she just stood out wherever she went. She always held herself so beautifully. She was a wonderful woman, but she could sometimes be hard on us too. If we didn't measure up we certainly heard about it or copped it.

I wasn't a fearless child but I pretended to be. I had a bit of an aggressive streak. It was like a protective mechanism, a big cover-up, because I was very fat and people laughed at me. So I used my aggression. I might not have been able to run as fast as some but I could certainly use my mouth to deflect attention. My father always wanted a boy and for many years I was made to have my hair cut like a boy.

When I was about 12 my mother took me to the barber and he refused to cut my hair like that again.

I can never remember my father putting his arm around any of us, but I never stopped loving him — even though his behaviour was abusive and I wanted it to stop. I believe the war had something to do with the way he was. One of his sisters told me that before my father went to war he was a fun-loving brother and a wonderful son, but when he came back he had changed. He saw his brother killed overseas and that would have been traumatic for a young man in his early twenties. I've seen loving, kind letters my father wrote to his mother while he was away at the war and I'd never have thought my father would have known how to express himself like that.

At the time we were getting hidings and seeing what happened to our mother we didn't talk about it. It was just the way things were. Then for years after we still didn't talk about the violence we grew up with. Recently I said to my older sister, 'Why didn't we talk about it?' and she just shrugged her shoulders and said, 'What's to talk about? We survived.' And I thought, 'Well yes, we did survive,' but I think what you see and hear as children lives within you. I feel it has affected me.

I've had a lot of different experiences in my life but I suppose everything along the way has been character building, if you want to look at it like that. When I was 21 I married a Swiss and went to live in his country. I think the fact that I went away as a young girl helped me to cope with my childhood. The sadness for me was leaving my mother and hoping that nothing would happen to her while I was away.

That relationship didn't work out, although I was with my husband for several years. I remember writing to my mother to say I was going to come home without my husband. She wrote me back the saddest letter I've ever received. She said, 'Compared to what I've had you just don't know how lucky you are.' She told me that she had never known a kind word for a meal she'd prepared and had never had my father put his arm around her. I never knew how hard it had been for her because when you're growing up you're not particularly concerned about the needs of your mum. What she was saying in her letter was, 'Think very carefully about leaving,' but of course you look at things from your own point of view and I wanted to come back to New Zealand, so I did.

My second marriage was to a man with four children. I'm sorry that marriage ever happened. I loved my husband but I didn't want the children. The biological link just wasn't there. We had two children living with us for a few years so that was very difficult. In these situations there's the assumption of, 'Love me, love my kids,' but it's not that easy. You've got to want to do that. I shouldn't have gone into that marriage knowing how I was feeling. Children sense when they're not wanted. Part of the problem was I actually resented the attention my husband gave to his children. That's a terrible thing really! They had every right. Even though I was really hard on them, the children have turned out wonderfully. I still feel bad about it but I suppose that experience has been part of my growth and journey too.

I'm now very happily married. I truly love my husband and he certainly loves me. Theo has been brought up so very differently to me. He's Tuhoe and his first language is Maori. He is a very spiritual man. He prays in a very conversational way to God. It's so beautiful. He'll just say in Maori, 'Look, I'm sorry to bug you Lord. I know everyone else is on to you today, but I've got this issue . . .' I never expected to fall in love with this man. The first time I met him he looked very nondescript, but after a while I looked at him with interest and I started to see something there that I actually didn't see at first, and I thought, 'What a fine, distinguished man.' Then I realised, 'What a fine man inside.'

When we first got together I said, 'We're so different, why are you with me?' He said, 'You've got something to do with your life. My tupuna have put me beside you to help you with that work.' That took me by surprise! I had no idea what he was talking about. I thought, 'How off the wall can you be?' I didn't want to be out there raising the flag. All I wanted to do was have a good time and smell the roses.

In those early days I asked Theo to teach me the Maori language but he said, 'No, what you need to learn first are the tikanga, the Maori values, and that's what I'll teach you. In time you will know the difference. You will notice, Merepeka, when people stand up to talk that while they have the language it's sometimes not based on the values,' And that's very true. I listen to how some Maori people talk and what they say is quite hurtful. Sometimes my spirit gets wounded. Theo has always said to me, 'You must never do that. You must always leave a person with dignity. You've got to base everything on values and make decisions which are based on what is good for the people.'

Theo has spent the last thirteen years demonstrating those values to me. He's taught me that there are always two ways of saying things. One way you'll be remembered for how you said it and the other you'll be remembered because of what you've said. You don't want to be remembered for how you said it, which could be the quite dogmatic or thump the table way. You want to be remembered for the message of hope or encouragement or support you gave or just the fact that you've stated a view well.

If I look back I've probably always spoken out but I know I used to be quite blunt and I think my manner would have been off-putting for some people. I sometimes came across in an aggressive way. I'm sad about that now, but at the time I didn't know any better. Now I really cringe inside when I think of the way I sometimes acted. But then again, you learn from your mistakes and you go on. Once I had the awareness about my behaviour it wasn't hard to change, and my family has said that I'm a much better person now.

I've always been quite strong and determined. I suppose I try to be fearless. I have no problem holding a different view from others and stating it. I think if you know what you're talking about and if you state it clearly, people will listen to you. They might not agree with you, but I believe most people respect a person who is putting their case strongly and has the conviction to talk about it. There are some people I don't agree with at all, but I just enjoy the fact that they've actually stated their view so we can have a discussion about the issues.

My two sisters are just like I am and whenever we meet we tend to debate or discuss issues. You've got to know what you're talking about because there's not much room for small talk. I think our husbands get a little bit annoyed and either go off and play golf or retire to the television lounge because our conversations are so in-depth.

I usually just let things happen rather than setting goals but about five years ago an American woman I was working with said, 'Look Merepeka we do all of this strategic planning for our businesses, what about your personal strategic planning?' I said, 'I haven't thought about it,' and she said, 'Well you should because otherwise it's hit and miss. Even though you still might eventually get where you want to go, why not take a direct route?' So I set about seven goals. At the time I put them aside but I've actually achieved them all now.

One of my goals was to lose weight. I used to be a big woman, about a size 26. One day my knee was playing up and I'd heard that people could get cortisone injections so I went to the doctor and asked for one. She just looked at me and said, 'With your size that's merely the start of it,' and I was a bit taken aback. She said, 'Look, you're a Maori woman. You're under stress, running around here, there and everywhere. You're heart attack material. If you don't do something about your weight, you'll be dead in five years.'

So I did do something. I went to a dietitian at the hospital and went on a diet and walked everywhere. They said they thought it would take three years to lose my weight but I did it in two and I feel quite proud of that achievement. I believe because I'm small now doors have opened to me that should have been open a long time ago. There's a prejudice towards people who are big. People don't take you seriously. They think you've got no self-discipline or you're lazy. I don't think that's true at all! When you're big you work just as hard as anybody else.

My life has been full on for twenty years. I haven't really stopped. I had a number of businesses I went into undercapitalised. When you do that you end up doing two or three jobs instead of paying a staff member. Even now that I'm not in business, I'm doing this job which is full on. I've realised self-care is really very important, probably more than ever, but I don't usually get time to myself. What energises me is beauty in people. I'm not talking about their looks. I'm talking about the words they say and how they say them. I find good music uplifting. I love the classics and I find beauty in artwork. But there hasn't been any real self-care for a long time and that's something I need to look at.

My mother died a few months ago and I haven't grieved for her yet because I haven't had time. I went to a rally in Hastings recently and Alan Duff had read in the paper that I was coming. He rang me and invited me to have a drink with some of the Books in Schools trustees. Although I'd only met him once before very briefly, he invited me to stay with his family in their beautiful home in Havelock North. That was really lovely. The next day they were flying off to Australia and he said, 'There's the keys to the house and there's the car. Stay for however long you like.' I'd actually intended to go back to Wellington to write a report and he said, 'The computer's there.' So I did stay the weekend because it felt very right. What Alan did was exhibit true manaakitanga, which is basically about making me welcome. He didn't talk about it. He just did it. It was there in the still and the quietness, when I could have some peace on my own, I started to grieve for my mum. I'm really grateful to Alan for that.

Sometimes I do feel like I need a break. I said to Theo recently, 'Darling, it'll be lovely when I can just do nothing. I'm looking forward to the day when I can stop and smell the roses,' and he said, 'You'll be bored stiff in three weeks.' I don't know why I didn't just take a nice quiet job where I could earn my money and go home and switch off but I don't think I was destined for that. I'm actually becoming quite resigned to the fact that there probably is a leadership role I'm going to play. People are saying to me that I should be going into politics and I hope I can resist that.

The other night Theo and I were lying in bed, it was very early in the morning and we often talk and he prays at that time. I said to him, 'Is this it Theo? Is this the work you talked about me doing? Am I there yet?' And he said, 'No dear, it's only the beginning.' So smelling the roses is definitely out! I don't quite know what's in store for me, but I dare say I'm not going to go back and just live quietly in Rotorua when my contract at Refuge is finished. There's still a lot of work to be done.

Merepeka's message

To women who have a dream they want to follow, above all things be honest. Now is the time for honesty — honesty in relationships, in dealing with other people, in what we say and write. I think if we're honest we can't go far wrong.

And I'd say be flexible. Everyone these days is talking about taking a planned approach to your future and if I was starting off again I'd quite possibly do that, but even in a planned approach you've got to allow for some flexibility. You've got to allow for the thing that's going to come right out of left-field. It might send you off in a whole different direction, but it could well be the direction you never thought to look, and that may be where your dream and your future lie. Theo definitely came out of left-field for me. I said to him once, 'Oh darling I wish I could have met you twenty years ago,' and he said, 'Twenty years ago I wasn't right for you.' And he's right. So what I'm saying is sometimes something unexpected will come into your life that is just right for you, and I believe you'll know it when it comes.

Sukhi Turner

'It's best to be upfront and forthright and not to mislead people.'

Sukhi Turner was elected as the first woman mayor of Dunedin in 1995. As a woman who is committed to environmental issues and holds strong community values, Sukhi has boldly challenged the more conservative, right-wing views of her fellow councillors and weathered the resulting storms.

Born in Northern India, Sukhi attended an Anglican boarding school in the foot of the Himalayas and grew up speaking three languages: Hindi, Punjabi and English. Later she went to America on an exchange scholarship and studied history and political science. In 1969 Sukhi met New Zealand cricketer Glenn Turner at a function in India and married him when she was 21, four years later. Eventually the family settled in Dunedin. Sukhi's involvement in kindergarten committees, school boards of trustees, parent teacher associations and her interest in community issues led her naturally into a career in politics. She has two adult children and lives with her family in Dunedin.

When I first came to New Zealand in 1973 I would never have imagined that one day I would be the mayor of Dunedin. I can remember the first year I came here. My husband Glenn had made 1000 runs in the first half of the English County season, which was a particularly important feat in the cricketing world. He was given a reception by the mayor and councillors in the municipal chambers and I was given Shona McFarlane's book on Dunedin, which at once gave me a reference about the city. I became aware of what was around me and very interested and Dunedin just grew on me from there.

I see myself as a bit of a change agent. I believe in changing things for the better — constant improvement in one's self and in society. In a way I'm a bit restless. I've always been used to change. My father was in the Indian Air Force when I was a child so we moved around a lot. Also there was a big shift for me when I was sent to my grandparents when I was 9 months old because my mother had three children within the space of three years. It's quite a tradition for grandparents to help out in these circumstances. I was with them until I was 6 years old. Then my father was concerned because I was living in a village and he felt it was time for me to come to an urban area and go to a proper school. That was quite a big change at that stage, having to then come and stamp my place in the family next to the three other siblings.

I can remember my first day in a big city school, everything was so different. Instead of sitting on a mat, we actually had tables and chairs. We moved often. The travel always made me quite aware of change. I was interested in the world but the one thing I didn't like was having to lose the environment I had become comfortable in.

The only stable, long-term thing was that we went to the same boarding school every year in the same place and I enjoyed that. My first day at boarding school one young person tried to bully me and I stood up to that and said, 'You can't push me around.' I just wouldn't have it! That was a valuable lesson. From that I learned that you can stand up for yourself. I think that made me more sure of myself.

As a young woman I was quite westernised in a way. I'd gone to an English-speaking school in India, I'd been to England and had travelled in Egypt. After my education in India I went to the States for three years on an exchange scholarship and I decided I wanted to graduate from the States rather than from India. It was a far more liberal and far more outward-looking education and that suited me. Universities in India were still very, very traditional.

I'm someone who challenges tradition a bit and is not scared to do that if I think I'm right. My parents thought I was going to have a marriage that was arranged in India but I met Glenn and wanted to marry him. It was definitely a heart decision for me. I was very much in love and I thought that Glenn would be my life partner and it was mutual. I just felt that it was right. I was very determined. I guess it was quite radical but you never really realise how radical you are until you think back. I just knew that was what I wanted to do and I was quite insistent about it.

My father especially was very distressed. I told him a year before I graduated that I knew this young fellow from New Zealand and that I would like them to meet him. I was only about 20 then. My father said throughout the year that he just wanted me to concentrate on my studies and finish my degree then he would think about it. There was quite a lot of correspondence. I tried to persuade him and in the end I think it was my mother who said they really should meet Glenn. After they met him they decided he wasn't the kind of person who might get married and then divorced the next year. Because that was another thing that was so different, the cultural values around family life and marriage. My father also worried that Glenn wouldn't be able to provide for me. Those were the days when the man provided for the woman and they couldn't believe you could actually earn money as a cricketer. Eventually I got married in England and for the first years of the marriage we travelled because of Glenn's cricket. My early life gave me good training for the kind of travel I did then. We settled in Dunedin when our children just started school.

I became interested in local government affairs in 1989. My children were getting older and I felt I had more time to be involved in civic matters and I'd always been interested in politics. Before that I had been involved in quite a lot of community activities through schools, right from kindergarten to primary schools and secondary schools. I was also interested in our neighbourhood support group. So becoming involved in local politics was just a logical progression.

I'm quite an outspoken person and I'm not afraid of conflict but that hasn't been always the case. When I was on school committees it took me some time to actually get the courage to say things that might not be supported by other people – to stand up and be counted. There was a turning point for me at a school committee meeting. I can't remember the actual issue but I felt really passionately about it, strong enough to actually stand up and say so, even though I was nervous.

Once I'd actually broken that barrier I did become more confident; that was a good lesson because my view was in the minority and I found that it was valid. So when I finally got into council I felt that it was alright to say things that you might not get majority support for. I've always believed that you should be able to take some risks, despite the fact people might not agree. I think it's very important in politics not to fudge the issues. It's best to be upfront and forthright and not to mislead people. At times this has made me unpopular with some people.

In the council if I felt differently about things I'd say so. As a result the paper always picked it up. The media always tends to focus on things that might be a wee bit different so I used to feature quite regularly. I did get a lot of flak from my fellow councillors, but the public endorsed me overwhelmingly, because a year before the election in 1995 I decided I'd stand for the mayoralty and I was elected.

When I ran for mayor I had a really strong belief that I could do it. I felt I had the ability and the confidence and the issues to run with and I felt there needed to be a change in the way we did things. I genuinely felt that things needed to be better. I wanted to see Dunedin as the most environmentally friendly, humane and people-centred city and a community which gives opportunities to all and has a great feeling of belonging.

I learnt quite a salutary lesson in my first term as mayor when one of my councillors was quite upset about the way I was doing things. I had had the courage to speak my mind and it had certainly upset a certain fairly powerful section of our council – the old boys. I was actually saying things that were ringing true and that upset some of these powerful people. There was an emergency motion brought to council to say that I could only talk on things council had agreed on and that I couldn't actually talk on issues I believed in. It was one of these political game plans people play and it was quite out of order, because it went against the mandate the mayor receives by being elected at large.

It created a lot of publicity. We had all the television cameras down from TVNZ and TV3 and they did a *20/20* documentary. I knew I could go at this head on and escalate it because how dare anyone bring a motion which basically gags me? Is this not a democracy? Do we not have freedom of speech? Instead I chose to diffuse the process by acknowledging that some of the comments I'd made might have upset a few people. As a result the motion was withdrawn. When I was voted in as mayor for a second term it was quite satisfying personally because it showed people still had confidence in me.

One thing I feel really strongly about is that there's no need in the political arena to become vindictive and personalise things. There are people you don't like because they have different ideas to you but that doesn't mean you put them down. When I've been attacked I see that it is my ideas the opposition is attacking so I never take it personally. You can't afford to! I think the democratic process is all about thrashing things out, not attacking actual personalities. I usually handle conflict head on. I won't suffer bullies. If I think that someone is confrontational and is coming at me then I'm quite ready to stand up and say, 'Watch it mate.' So in a way I am quite combative initially. Then I need to stop and think how I'd like to actually handle the situation and find a way through.

It's important to have the capacity to be able to absorb the different points of views and I think that makes for a good representative. No one person has all the answers. One of my failings is that I can be quite certain of things and quite dogmatic at times. But unless you are certain how can you actually pursue and be passionate about something? It's finding a balance and that is something I'm learning as I go.

I think that it's important to have some self-doubt because unless you have that you can think you're invincible and no one is. Sometimes when you're in a position like mine, with some influence and some power, you have to search yourself and ask, 'How could I have done that better?' Unless you have those doubts how do you listen to other people's good ideas, because you always say to yourself you're the fountain of all knowledge.

There are times when there is conflict I just sidestep because I don't think it's worth it, but if someone attacks my integrity and is saying I'm a bad person then I think that needs to be answered. If there's a criticism with me personally I try to see first of all if it's valid and then do something about it. If you have a bad relationship with someone you care about I don't think that's good for your wellbeing. If there are misunderstandings you need to talk them out and sometimes it takes a while. There was a time when I would have said, 'I thrive on conflict. It gives me a buzz! Gets my adrenaline going.' But I don't think basically in the long run that it's very good for you. I think you can get a better buzz out of working collaboratively with people.

I believe we should give of our time and our talents. There are some people who are better equipped than others because they have more privileges. I think it's incumbent on those who do have the power and influence to improve our culture. Certain sections of our society are community-minded and they give a hell of a lot, but unfortunately there has been a rise in this dreadful belief in the survival of the fittest and I feel passionate about challenging that. I think everyone should have responsibility for themselves but they should also feel that they have a responsibility to others as well. That 'me' culture is really quite detrimental. I think we have a responsibility to care for each other when we live in a society. I feel really strongly about that.

Sukhi's message

It's important to stand up for what you believe, even if you're afraid. That way you'll become more sure of yourself and when you're confident you've got a lot of courage and enthusiasm and you know you're going in the right direction and you're very focused. To achieve your goals you need that focus. I think you need to follow your heart and what seems right for you but first be sure that your heart is saying the right thing. So be a bit balanced about it. Sometimes in your life you might think you've been dealt the wrong cards, but often the negatives can be made into positives. You can say, 'What can I actually learn from this? How can this negative thing be transformed into something positive?' because there's always that possibility. So always be hopeful!

GATHERING SUPPORT

When the best and highest in us engages openly and honestly with the best and highest in others, there is fire.

The Power Principle, Blaine Lee

While the extent of our personal effort is of primary importance in the success of our endeavours, other peoples' input is also vital. Ideally, when we have a dream we have a team of people around us who will enthuse, uplift, advise, assist and ultimately celebrate our achievements with us. No matter how self-sufficient we are, there is no substitute for an encouraging word, offer of a helping hand, timely piece of advice, wise word of caution, generous favour or sincere praise. The bigger our dream, the more support we are likely to require.

If we lack sufficient support we can become proactive about bringing more positive and nurturing people into our life. There are numerous people who would love to get to know us and support us, but it is up to us to establish the contacts and build these relationships. High achievers usually recognise the importance of relationships and have developed the ability to surround themselves with like-minded, optimistic people who believe their dreams are possible. They are often friendly, warm and helpful and able to engage others and make them feel respected and valued. Needless to say the more we develop our interpersonal skills, the more we will attract encouraging people into our life.

If we share our passion about our ideas other people's interest will be captured. Often it's possible to generate support by sharing our vision, asking others for their ideas and feedback, giving them progress reports and showing appreciation for any help they give. Generally people are generous and love to share their knowledge and help others get ahead. Sometimes it's just a matter of plucking up the courage to ask. When we risk asking, we risk a refusal, but if we do get a 'no' we can always ask someone else. If we keep asking we will find people who are willing to give us the support we seek. It is however important to be selective in who we approach. Pessimistic people who are intent on pushing their dire predictions are best avoided. We need to protect our precious dreams from this kind of negativity.

Many people find having a mentor invaluable. This is usually someone they identify as having more experience than them, who is willing to offer ideas, support, feedback and advice on how to overcome challenges and take positive steps. Alternatively some people approach someone in a similar position to themselves and make a reciprocal arrangement to share information and work together on ideas and strategies for pursuing goals.

Another possibility is to obtain the services of a life coach. This person will clarify with us what we would like to achieve in the various aspects of our life, help us set realistic goals, be our cheerleader and delight in our successes. The consistency, focus and positivity of this relationship can help to propel us swiftly towards our dreams.

Having a wide range of contacts can also provide us with vital support. There are countless possibilities for increasing our personal and professional networks. Friendships and business contacts can be developed through the numerous groups bringing people together for the purposes of professional support, sports, hobbies, addressing social issues, learning or volunteer work. People we meet through these sources can often assist us in our achievements in unexpected and wonderful ways.

Sometimes, when our dreams go well beyond what we alone are capable of achieving, it is necessary to involve others by evoking their commitment and passion. Combining with other people to work on a shared vision can be stimulating and satisfying. June Mariu and Sue Kedgley are women of vision. Their ability to inspire others, generate support for their ideas and work closely with a team of like-minded people has enabled them to achieve much.

June Mariu

' . . .you can't make things happen by yourself. You have to
have people around you who go along with your vision . . .'

*June is affectionately known as Auntie or 'Mrs M' to
the kids of West Auckland. A woman of vision, June
has devoted forty-eight years of her life to working to
improve her community. A QSM recipient, June's quiet
but determined strength has enabled her to inspire others
to work with her to help bring her visions into reality.*

*June grew up at Hicks Bay, or Cape Runaway, on
the East Coast. Her parents fostered numerous children, instilling in her the values of caring and sharing.
June qualified as a teacher in 1952 then moved to
Auckland to pursue her passion for netball. She cap-
tained the New Zealand team in 1960. June and her
husband moved to Te Atatu when it was a very new
suburb with the attendant social problems. June was involved in reviving the Maori
Women's Welfare League and was the national President from 1987–1990.*

*June was on the staff of Rutherford High from 1972 until 1987. In 1982, as
the senior mistress, she was aware the education system often failed to meet the needs
of Maori children. Passionate about helping children develop a sense of pride, June
set about establishing the Te Kotuku marae in the school. Her goal to create a
'living' marae has been realised with numerous programmes successfully running
from the marae.*

*June was widowed in 1986. She currently chairs the Te Whanau O Waipareira
Trust and Aotearoa Maori Netball Association and works with Te Puni Kokiri Maori
Development. She still lives in Te Atatu and has two adult children.*

I was brought up to care not just for my immediate family but for
those not so fortunate, so I guess I'm inclined to embrace the people
around me who get involved with me. I'm the one who has the visions and I'm lucky to get people to go along with them and so we
work it together. There are a lot of people on the same wavelength as

I am and that's really good because I feel that they're with me and I'm on the right track and I'm not the only one who sees it that way. Because if I was it could be very lonely. I'd think that maybe my visions are way out, but they don't seem to be.

My broad vision is for an equal and just society where communities are working together and that's what I'm committed to working for. The dream is that different cultures and levels of the community understand each other and there is harmony between them. You work for your community to create a better society. Maori people are facing so many difficulties. I believe if things are going right for the Maori people then they'll go right for the community as well. We'll play our part equally. All sorts of changes need to be made in the systems for us to achieve that. We're saying that loud and clear at the moment. We're saying: 'Let us have a go! Maori issues dealt with by Maori, for Maori. Let us take responsibility and if we still foul it up then there's nobody to blame but ourselves.' I'm not saying that everybody else is to blame. Heavens no! We've got a whole lot of issues we need to work on and at the moment we're looking for how to make things better.

My vision of caring for others began as a child. We only had three in our family and that was a small family for Maori in those days, so my parents fostered children who were referred by the Social Welfare and they were brought up with us. I think we had about thirty-five kids come and stay, some of them until they were grown up, and my parents guided them. They were part of our family and I appreciated having all these kids come through with all of us taking an interest in each other.

When I really look back on my childhood the major lesson was that it's quite easy to embrace lots of people. It was just an automatic thing to care for and to pitch in and it's still like that. We achieve things through working together. My mum was a role model because I saw that she cared for people. She broadened our family and the responsibility to care for us and guide us was mainly on her. My dad worked and was there to support as well.

It's always challenging when you care about people to see that you do your best for them. I can't stand seeing anyone being put down or suffering. If I do I just step in and challenge. I'd try and take that person away until we see what can be done. I couldn't do anything else. In the past I've made myself unpopular like this, but it has worked out eventually. When things have calmed down other people realise why you did what you did. I really feel the person is what is important and we'll work through the rest after that, so it doesn't worry me to be unpopular in that situation. I know it'll sort itself out and if it doesn't, well tough. I did what I had to do and that's me.

Underlying all I do is my aim for total wellbeing for Maori people. I've been quite involved with that through Maori netball. I always loved netball and that's why I picked it as the way to address health. I was able to start Maori netball because I had played netball myself for New Zealand in the mainstream. I knew a lot of people and I was able to tap in, so that they made it happen. At first it was seen as segregation. Friends looked at me sideways when I wanted to start our own netball but I could see that netball was a way of getting young Maori women to address their health. To be champion netballers you need to have good wind, so smoking wasn't a part of that. I wasn't into lecturing. I don't think that always goes over well. Saying, 'Hey don't smoke', is not being square. It's about health! It's cool not to smoke.

So through the Maori netball I was able to work towards other aims like the total physical wellbeing of people. What I believe is that we need to think about what's good for us. If you haven't got good health you can't play any sports and you can't give of your best at school. If you don't work hard to get educated you can't get a good job. So it all links together. It's just common sense really.

We arranged for people to come and talk at one of our big netball gatherings to inspire the girls. Chick Cooper came and spoke and she was dynamic. She had a breast removed and she told them about how she wished there were people like the Maori Netball Association when she was younger because she had smoked like a chimney. Then she lifted her shirt up and showed where she'd had her breast removed. That was the most absolutely dramatic moment for those girls. They were just spellbound. She told them if she'd had people like those who were running Maori netball take an interest in her, maybe she wouldn't have lost her breast. It really had a massive effect. We can only make young people aware and then it's over to them after that. She was really lovely. She said, 'I'm not going to show you the other one because you'll be jealous.'

Something else I've been passionate about is the Maori Club at Rutherford High School. When I was teaching there I believed we needed to have a Department of Maori Studies, so I talked the head-master into it. It was important to get the teachers on board too and convince them we have much to offer, that the academic scene isn't the be all and end all. There are other things we can share. As a teacher you need to find ways of making these dreams really happen. I've done that by having people work with me. You have to plan it. I asked to use a couple of prefabs that had become redundant for a marae. Anyway I sort of tussled over these two buildings with the Phys Ed guy who wanted them too. The marae is standing there now so I obviously won. It was a very important dream for me because I could see a real need.

We were one of the first schools to have a marae. The aim has been to make it a living marae and I believe we've achieved that. We've got all sorts of programmes running there. This marae is the physical evidence of a dream. It's a place where we teach people to care for each other and work together. We teach Maori language there and have programmes like catering, hospitality courses, sew-ing and computer courses and Maori fashion. It's all part of it. We've got a lovely Kohanga Reo for the little ones and we've got a Maori Performing Arts Programme.

We've also got a programme we call Te Tangata where community people help the kids in the classrooms and give them an ear to listen if they're not feeling too good. Then the kids begin to realise that they care. It's all about helping kids to develop a pride in themselves – to stand tall and know they're good at certain things, so now be good at your school work, be good at your relationships with people. Parents need support too. They need to feel good about themselves and at times that's really hard if you're not employed and if you haven't been very well educated.

We are trying to remedy this business of low achievement and truancy. With truancy comes all sorts of other things. The idea is to work in with whoever we can, with whatever expertise we can get, people who are really looking at how we can stop this drug scene because it's having an effect. So it's a matter of bringing people together to work with them to achieve our goals for a better community.

The basic words we use are *awhi* – embrace, and to have *aroha* – to love one another, to *tiaki* – to take care of each other, to *tautoko* – to support each other and to *maanaki* – to look after people. Those are key words for me. They're the base of everything I have anything to do with. These are the values I come back to always. We sort of share them with everybody. That's where it's at. It works! You have your moments when there's conflict and things go haywire, but that's life. If you're strong in those values there's always a way of making things come right. Sport and music and dance are good things for peace, for sharing with other people, because you forget any barriers. Those things build positive relationships with everybody.

Spirituality is a personal issue for people. I always go to church when I go home to the East Coast. I love the services because my cousin has this lovely organ and we have really swinging church services. I can't just go to church for the sake of it, I have to respect the messenger and enjoy the service. There has to be a message for me to reinforce that what I'm doing matters. I believe if you're doing your best for your neighbours that's Christian.

I can remember as a kid looking at the moon and praying for a black horse of my own. I forget what I was saying but I was really fervently praying to that moon that I wanted a black horse. It so happened that there was a black pony and my dad gave it to me. So I've always believed prayers get answered. There is somebody out there who listens who can make things happen. It's a matter of trying to be morally upright and doing what you can for those around you.

June's message

I'd say if you've got a dream, go all out for it. Don't let go of it, because there's nothing more satisfying than to see it happen. Then you know it was worth all the effort. It would be a disappointment if you didn't have a go when you really would have liked to try. Whatever I've wanted to do I've always had a go. I think it's because we were told at school to go for our dreams and goals and try to achieve what we wanted. Having had the experience with the Maori Women's Welfare League of walking down the corridors of Parliament because of what I believe and going in to visit ministers of the crown to let them know how they could use us in creating wellbeing for our people, I know it is possible to make a difference. Although I'm a person who has had big visions, they have become a reality only because of other people's involvement. It hasn't just been me. I really want to stress that.

You're the dreamer but you can't make things happen by yourself. You have to have people around you who go along with your vision or think the same way you do and are involved with the same things as you. So talk to people who might help you make the dream come true and get their help. That help is where you can get your strength.

Sue Kedgley

'If you're going to try to change things you need to work with a group of dedicated people.'

Sue is a well-known Green Member of Parliament, writer and campaigner on social issues dear to her heart. Her interest in healthy eating has led to her passion for raising people's awareness about what is really in the food we eat, genetic engineering and creating change on these issues. In 1994 Sue, together with three others, started the Safe Food Campaign, an organisation which now has over 600 members throughout the country.

Sue grew up in Wellington. By the time she had completed an MA in Political Science at age 22, she was one of the founding members of the women's liberation movement in this country and had coauthored Sexist Society, a book on the women's movement. A trip to Boston to attend a women's liberation conference in 1973 resulted in her staying in New York for the following eight years. During this time Sue worked in the Women's Secretariat of the United Nations and as a special assistant to the Assistant Secretary for Economic and Social Affairs. On returning to New Zealand Sue worked as a current affairs reporter, television director, producer and writer. She has written seven books, her latest being Eating Safely in a Toxic World.

Sue became a Wellington City Councillor in 1992 and a Member of Parliament in 1999, and sees her entry into Parliament as an opportunity to continue to work towards the environmental changes she feels so strongly about. She lives in Wellington with her husband Denis Foot and son Zac.

I have had an interesting life but I've never sat down with a piece of paper and worked out where I wanted to go or how to get there. It's been more about creating and responding to opportunities really. A lot of it's been by luck. Like getting into Parliament, you could say that was a fluke, but if I hadn't got in I would have carried on pursuing the same issues anyway outside of Parliament. Some people say you create your own reality and I really think that you do on some level. If I've got a very clear idea I often find it tends to happen anyway even if I don't personally initiate things.

For most of my life I've been involved in political action and trying to change things. My focus at the moment is safe food issues, preventative health, animal welfare, gaining recognition for complementary health care and other issues. I am actually a very focused person. I have very clear objectives about what I want to achieve. I'm always reading and researching and thinking, trying to work out how I can get things changed. It's not easy. Even though I'm now in Parliament the opportunities are quite limited. You can't just wave a wand and change things overnight.

I guess my life has been about doing the things that come naturally to me rather than consciously figuring out where my skills lie. I really enjoy communicating and raising people's awareness, whether it's through writing books or speaking to groups, and in the political context trying to figure out how to change things. If I look back, those are the main areas I've been involved in most of the time. Some people are very, very good at beavering away and researching in a particular area but I prefer putting all the pieces of the jigsaw together and seeing the big picture. I'm not a details person at all.

A lot of the changes in my career have happened because of outside opportunities or by following my instinct or a hunch. In the early days I helped set up the Women's Liberation Movement, as it was then called. I felt very passionately about the way women were treated then and expected to live their lives through men. The world at that stage revolved around men, and women were expected to spend their lives looking after men and children, not following their dreams or doing anything in their own right.

In 1973 I decided to go to an international feminist conference in Boston. I got to New York and I just loved the whole energy and excitement of the place. I really wanted to stay in New York and I managed to get myself a job as a journalist covering the General Assembly of the United Nations. After three months I got a job in the Women's Secretariat of the UN. That was an ideal job because I was paid to work on the issues that preoccupied me at that stage.

I came back from New York in 1981, after eight years at the UN, because my parents had a car accident. I took a year's leave from the UN and that was a turning point – either I'd stay in New York for the rest of my life, as many of my friends have, or I'd come back to live in New Zealand. I always felt like a permanent transient in New York. Also I was ready to leave the United Nations because I wasn't really interested in moving up through the ranks of a bureaucracy. To do that you have to be prepared to conform, censor yourself and fit into the corporate world. I could see very clearly how you could get ahead but you would have to very much abide by the rules and play the game. I've never been interested in doing that. I'm interested in pursuing ideas and promoting issues, not climbing the hierarchy.

So I came back to New Zealand and worked as a television journalist. I loved ferreting around as a reporter and dealing in depth with different issues. Then various people persuaded me to apply for the Television Directors and Producers Training Course. It had a lot of status and it was assumed to be the ultimate thing that everyone in television would want to do. So although I loved being a reporter I did this training and it was like a military camp. I didn't enjoy the training and I didn't enjoy being a director either. It's one of the only times in my life that I've gone along with what other people suggested and not followed my own instincts. It's a good example of what happens if you don't follow your heart. For some reason I didn't go back and say, 'I'm not cut out to be a director, I want to go back to being a reporter.' Instead I left television. It's one of the few regrets I have in my career, although I did make quite a few documentaries as an independent film-maker after that.

I had a pretty good balance in my life in the nineties. I married late and after my son Zac was born in 1990, when I was 42, I spent a few years at home writing. I had started my book *Mum's The Word* when a friend rang and asked me if I'd stand for the Wellington City Council for the Green Party. At the time I said, 'Maybe next time.' I've always been interested in politics but I was busy writing the book and looking after my child so I wasn't quite ready. Then oddly enough I dreamed quite vividly for the next three nights that I was standing as a Green for the Wellington City Council. I figured that maybe something was trying to tell me I should stand, so I did. Working as a councillor was really a very good experience, until the last few years, when it became highly political and quite unpleasant.

Around this time about five of us decided to set up the Safe Food Campaign. After a while we realised it was very difficult trying to communicate these issues through the media because they're quite complex and a couple of column inches in a newspaper was not enough. We decided we needed to write a book. Before I got around to looking for a publisher, a publisher rang me and asked whether I'd be interested in writing a book about safe food. It was almost like we put that idea out there and someone else picked it up.

Originally when we set up the Safe Food Campaign our focus was trying to change things through the political system. We did all this research and we took it off to the Minister of Health and pointed out to her that some additives in our food supply had been banned in other countries because they caused cancer in animals or had other harmful effects. But we got absolutely nowhere. So we shifted our focus to informing the consumer so they could make their own choices about what was safe to eat and increase the demand for organic produce. There's a wonderful bunch of women (and some men) running the Safe Food Campaign. One of my great satisfactions is that now that I've had to step aside to go into Parliament it's still going strong and other women are stepping into my role.

I ended up standing for Parliament because someone asked if I'd put myself on the Green Party List. I did so with some reluctance because Zac was just a bit young and I didn't want to ruin my family life. I was very happy when I was selected as sixth on the list. I never thought the Greens would get six people into Parliament. I thought they'd get four if they were lucky, so I had no expectation that I'd become an MP. On election night I was devastated that the Greens had missed out by such a tiny amount but I just got on with my life. Then suddenly we were in! I was in a state of shock for a couple of months but I'm gradually adapting and really enjoying being an MP. It's a great privilege and responsibility being part of the first Green caucus in Parliament.

I must admit it's difficult trying to reconcile being a mother, a wife and an MP – juggling all the demands on my time. It's exciting being out there and trying to change things in society and it's very easy for that to become all consuming. That is without question the most difficult area for me. My family, and in particular my son Zac, are more important to me than anything else, so one of the things I've had to do is learn how to say no. I get invitations to speak from all around New Zealand. I have to be quite disciplined and be careful I'm not getting completely out of balance and being away from my family too much. I'm very conscious that there are people in politics who are off out there trying to change the world while neglecting the whole area of their home life. I try hard to avoid doing that – not always with total success.

I've always had a very close group of women friends who have been a wonderful support over the years and that's been really important to me. One way or another I've always worked with groups of women, in the early days of the women's movement of course and ever since. The whole time I was at United Nations I was active in the women's group there. I was involved with a group of media women at Television New Zealand and then with some very supportive women on the Council and then with the Safe Food Campaign. If you're going to try to change things you need to work with a group of dedicated people. You can't do it on your own. I've also worked with a lot of young women and I really enjoy that. I try to help them get started in their careers by writing references or providing them with support and feedback about where they might want to go and how to get started.

Back in the seventies we wouldn't have imagined there would be a woman Prime Minister and Leader of the Opposition and Chief

Justice and so forth. In some areas we've finally broken the glass barriers and women can do everything and can run the nation and achieve whatever they set out to achieve. But there are still a whole lot of issues for women. As you solve one set of problems another set of problems emerge. I think for women the whole business of trying to balance their family and personal life is a big issue. Women are still doing the bulk of child rearing and running the home and are constantly under pressure because they are trying to succeed in paid work as well and haven't got any time for themselves. I think there's a tremendous number of women who are torn – who are having to go out to work when they'd really rather be home with their children. Many low income women earn a pittance. So there are lots and lots of issues out there.

Anyone who was involved in the early women's movement will agree that it was a fantastic experience. There was a great sense of solidarity – women working together and sharing common goals and a common vision. It was very inspiring. With virtually every movement in history there is a period when it has its most energy, when there are a whole set of injustices or things that need to be changed. As the movement gathers strength and succeeds in bringing about some of the change it loses some of its urgency. I think that's happened to the women's movement to some extent. At that early stage you needed collective action to change things. There's a feeling now that it's much more up to individual women. A lot of women think they can achieve things and solve their problems by themselves. I suspect that maybe in a few years time there may be another round of collective action.

At this stage I'm more concerned about how we are systematically destroying our environment and how all the life support systems of the planet are under threat. There's a view that the earth and the entire natural world belongs to us – that it's a sort of giant factory producing things for human consumption. We are entitled to use all the earth's natural resources and all other species for our own purposes and manipulate and genetically engineer them and experiment upon them. We're starting to reap the consequences of our material-ism, our rampant consumerism and our attitude to the earth. We are having to face the unpleasant reality that the earth is in a state of ecological crisis. These are the sorts of things I feel passionately about, and they are on top of my agenda at the moment.

Sue's message

I'm a strong believer in being involved in the things that really interest you. If you are on a bit of a treadmill and not enjoying what you're doing, sometimes it's a good idea to take some time out, to reassess what you really want to do. Some women I know who needed a change in direction gave themselves permission to take six months or so off to find out what they really wanted to do. They went off in a completely new direction as a result, and almost invariably they have been very successful. Obviously not every woman can take six months off to find out what she wants to do, but as much as possible I recommend that women follow their passion, because if you're doing something that you're interested in or you feel strongly about, you will get so much more satisfaction out of it, and probably be very successful at it too.

HEALING THE PAST

Emotions unregistered, unrecognised and unqueried –
emotional illiteracy – are costly.

Towards Emotional Literacy, Susie Orbach

Our life is shaped by our past experiences. If past disappointments and hurts are an impediment to our living life confidently and wholeheartedly then we need to take the time to address them. Many of us have issues from the past that still trouble us from time to time. People commonly try to deal with unfinished business by putting it behind them, putting on a brave face and moving on. This can work well in some situations but when the wound goes deep, avoiding facing the issues and attempting to deny hurtful memories usually does not make them go away. Instead they stay hidden inside, creating a heavy heart and a battered spirit. Our confidence, wellbeing and ability to relate effectively are undermined.

Energy that could go into creating exciting new ventures can be expended keeping unhappy memories at bay and struggling to cope with intense emotions. We may find ourselves often ruminating over painful incidents from the past, struggling with feelings such as sadness, hurt, anxiety, resentment or anger or trying to overcome a pervasive sense of inadequacy, worthlessness or shame. Past hurts make their presence felt when we encounter people and situations that remind us (often unconsciously) of earlier times. We find ourselves distressed and triggered into reacting to others in inappropriate or defensive ways.

Despite carrying an unhealed past we may still be a high achiever. Others may admire our competence, but behind our rather brittle coping facade we may feel like a fraud. Our mask of confidence hides a vulnerable person with low self-esteem and a harsh inner critic who berates us when we fail to measure up to our own high expectations. Our relationships with others may lack closeness because we withdraw or use aggression to protect our vulnerable self from further hurt.

We are likely to benefit from doing some healing work if our past persistently encroaches on our day-to-day life in these ways. The questions on page 253 will help you to access this. The way to gain freedom from past issues is to work through them. While we can do our best to control our self-defeating behaviour and develop techniques to overcome situations which challenge us, when we do this we are focused on managing our responses rather then addressing the underlying issues. When we deal with the real issues that are causing the distress we bring about permanent change.

There are many different ways to heal. Although it is sometimes possible to do our healing work informally by reading self-help books, journal writing and having discussions with friends, it is often more useful to seek professional help. Counselling or psychotherapy provides a caring, confidential and safe relationship. An effective counsellor will act as a guide on the healing journey, offering emotional support, insights, feedback and information. A variety of personal growth courses are also available in the community and most people find that each one they attend is another step in their healing.

Many successful people have experienced major adversities in their life and have emerged as compassionate, inspiring people. We can be enormously strengthened by the difficulties we have gone through when we take the time to understand and work through what has happened. It is then the gifts in these situations become apparent. Soala Wilson's story shows the strength of character and determination it is possible to develop when we take the time to heal our past.

Soala Wilson

' . . . my past does not equal my future.'

Soala owns and successfully manages The Works Hairdressing Salon which is based in a beautifully restored villa in Auckland. She was born in Samoa in 1959 and has lived in New Zealand since she was 10 years old.

As a child Soala lived with her family's alcoholism and abuse. She left school early but was determined to succeed, so returned when she was 19, as an adult student. A highly motivated and inspiring woman, Soala has spent years healing from her childhood hurts and pursuing her goals to the point where she now feels she is standing on a rock solid foundation and is able follow her passion: to challenge child abuse and domestic violence in our society.

Soala won the 1999 Pacific Businessperson of the Year award and when she claimed her award, Soala expressed the pain of her upbringing and challenged the Pacific Island culture to stop the emotional and physical abuse that still occurs. Soala is committed to inspiring people to change by continuing to speak out honestly about her life and sharing the wisdom she's gained.

With the background I grew up in, it's been survival but nowadays I see myself as a very strong person. I think the biggest thing for me has been that I just refuse to be a victim, refuse to settle for second best, refuse to be told I can't do it.

I was born in Samoa. It was a painful childhood, I was shifted from aunties to uncles . . . and I hated it. I felt like they didn't want us, but they felt obligated to look after us. I was always with my twin and my younger sister. All girls. Our aunties and uncles have large families themselves and then we were lumped onto them, just three other mouths to feed. They tried their best, but I felt I wasn't wanted there.

There was constant violence around. We'd often get hidings, sometimes even for making a murmur, being around — just being alive. I remember my cousin abusing my little sister. He'd light a match that would burn right down to a charcoal and he'd stick it onto the sole of her feet or burn the palm of her hand right into the skin. We were helpless. If we intervened we would get hit. I try to erase those memories and not get angry about it because it doesn't help me now.

The abuse affected me mentally and psychologically, I actually think it stunted my growth. Emotionally I had a lot of catching up to do in the last twenty-seven years. I was a very lonely child, very shy, very introverted — I didn't say anything. You know the theory of 'be seen and not heard'? Your opinion doesn't count. I often think that as a child you're born with a voice. You're a child of God, a child of the universe. Surely you should be able to speak? You have a soul in this little person. You may be a baby, but you have a spirit. You have a voice! If I could have spoken as a child I would have said, 'I hate this life!' Sometimes I'd think, 'Why did you have us if you don't acknowledge our existence? What's the point in living if you don't care for me?' Not just care as in providing, but in the emotional and spiritual sense. I guess that's where my grandmother came in.

She was my loving mum. She's the only one that made me feel that I belonged. She loved me unconditionally. I always cry when I talk about her. She didn't have much to offer in terms of material possessions. But she offered me love, purity, acceptance and respectability. I admired her. She had integrity. She was very solid in her belief in herself, a woman of her word and very respectful of other people. Unfortunately I didn't fully appreciate her when she was alive, but I've always believed that she was my foundation. From a baby to when I was about 7 or 8 that foundation was set for me. To be quite honest, I think it's her that's pushing me to speak out about child abuse and domestic violence now. I have to speak to honour her.

I was 10 when we came to New Zealand. When I was 13 there was a turning point in my life. My mother had been beaten up the night before, and she was so angry and I guess I must have just been around and alive and I was in the firing line, 'Soala, you're ugly and you're a stupid Samoan girl. You'll never make anything out of your life.' It was really shattering. I think everything just drained out of me. Then something just clicked in my mind. It was, 'You're not going to beat me. I'm going to make it. No matter what it takes.' I told myself I was going to be successful because I was going to prove my mother and everyone else wrong. The power of the mind! What you think and believe, you will achieve. I didn't know then that was one of the ingredients of being successful. That was the fuel that got me going. How I was going to do it I didn't know, but I was open to opportunities that were placed in front of me and I went looking for them.

When I think back, I had a lot of rubbish that was put on to me and that really affected me. It made me angry and that anger manifested in so many different ways. It really affected my health. And it affected how I related to other people. I felt like I had been short-changed, in a big way. I used to have this steel wall around me fending off anyone who would come close to me. But it wasn't until years later I connected the anger and the abuse.

I did know I had to sort myself out and get rid of all the rubbish that I used to call my can of worms. I'd open the can and think, 'Yuk, I don't want to deal with this.' When I discovered the book *Think and Grow Rich* by Napoleon Hill I thought, 'Great, he's going to tell me how to make money.' But he talked about how you've got to heal your soul, your spirit, your mind and release your anger to complete your healing.

My process on the healing path had a kick-start about fifteen years ago when I went to the Forum Course. I went because I was curious. I'd seen the change in some of my friends' lives and I thought, 'Maybe there's something there for me.' There I discovered that I wasn't alone. People were popping up telling my story and I kept thinking 'How on earth do they know about my life?'

It was very powerful. From there I started making decisions. That was the challenge. If you're not happy where you're living or in your job or your relationship, make a decision. At the end of the weekend not only did I change where I was living, I changed my job and my relationship.

I started counselling and I read lots of books like *You Can Heal Your Life* and *The Power is Within You* by Louise Hay. I call my healing my journey to freedom. It was very painful because I had to relive my hurtful childhood. Part of my self-counselling was to do journal writing. It was amazing! I look back now and I think, 'I wrote that. That's what I went through! That was the pain!' I wrote about my anger at Mum and Dad because they weren't the parents I wanted. They basically weren't there for me.

That anger had manifested as ovarian cysts. I went to a man who specialised in Chinese medicine for treatment and he said, 'You know Soala, I can only treat you for so much. You need to look at the emotional and spiritual connections and what this anger is telling you.' It was the last thing I wanted to hear, but there was truth in it. I knew exactly what he was saying. Since then I have let go of my anger because I don't need it anymore and I'm monitoring my health very carefully. I'm now in control of my life, my health, my finances — everything.

My partner Chrissie has played a large part in my healing. She's an old soul. She said to me thirteen years ago, 'Soala, you've got all the answers within you.' At the time I was too busy looking outside of myself for the answers. It was like she'd thrown me a lifeline but it was for me alone to swim to life. I kept thinking, 'What does she mean?', until I got more and more into developing me, getting rid of the rubbish and looking inside of myself. Then I understood.

You know when you find love you start to fly. Just having somebody care and love you. That's what was missing in my life — love. It's been the biggest ingredient in my healing, being loved, being cared for, being respected, being allowed to speak — self-discovery without being judged. It's the best. I couldn't ask for anything more. It's just all there. I believe everybody needs that.

My grandmother died about ten years ago. I guess that's when her spirit became more alive in me. I had to finish the journey for her. At the time I didn't want to know, but now I do. I'm ready for it because I feel comfortable with me. Completing my healing and forgiving, has enabled me to stand solid on my own foundation. I guess that I can now truly say I have no fear to speak out. My grandmother didn't have any fear, even though she was ostracised by family and extended family because she spoke out on the same issues I am now speaking out about. So I guess it's through my veins, it's through my spirit, it runs deep. If I don't speak her spirit will roar in the silence and I will never honour her life.

When my grandmother died I was in my bedroom and I felt a presence and I went to the kitchen to Chrissie and I said, 'Somebody's in my room and I feel really scared.' So she said, 'It's OK, don't be afraid. Go back in there with love in your heart and sit and just let your spirit be open.' I was shaking but I went and sat in my room and just listened. And I found it was my grandmother. Then the phone rang and it was my sister ringing to say that Gran had passed away. I said, 'I know, Gran has just come to me to tell me.' At that time I didn't know why she came to me. Now I know why. I have to speak for her.

To fully discover myself I needed to go back to Samoa. It was like a journey I had to do to find out, 'Which country do I call home?' What I found was New Zealand is home, but the connection to the spirit of that land was so powerful. It was like being in love, that emotion of being in love with God. And I realised that was what my grandmother had. She had this magic relationship with God. I didn't understand it as a child, but she had love, and that love was just unconditional. She was frustrated with her family, people and church but she forgave and loved her people until the day she died.

One morning, at 5 o'clock, everyone was asleep so I thought I'd just sneak out and go for a walk on the beach. It was just me and the beach and I found myself being overwhelmed by this emotion that was God. I knew that the only thing that is going to save humanity is love. We need to go back to our God, whatever we want to call it. It always goes back to love – love for self – and everything goes from there.

The last step of healing for me has been to forgive other people for what they've done to me. I needed to let that go because my past does not equal my future. The whole month building up to the Pacific Island Business Award night I played a forgiveness tape before I went to sleep. It was just amazing! Unbeknown to me, when I walked up to the platform to accept the award it was completion. I'd forgiven my family. I'd had my mother's voice ringing in my ears right up to then and it stopped. It was so liberating!

That night I couldn't sleep. I was busy forgiving the last people I needed to let go. I thought I had completed my list but more names kept flooding into my mind. I sat up until 4 o'clock completing that process. I hadn't realised I was still angry at a lot of people. Since then I'm more able to listen without judgment. I've found more compassion and tolerance.

I think I've always felt like I was being looked after by someone, whether it's a guardian angel, God or my higher power. Even now I feel like my grandmother is my guardian angel. She's really coaching and encouraging me. I'm more in tune with the spiritual side of myself now. I now believe that we are here for a reason and we all need to discover what our purpose is. I'm using the award to speak out. Before I used to complain about these issues, but Chrissie said to me, 'Stop complaining and do something about it. If you're not prepared to do something then shut up.' And five years ago I came across a saying of Gandhi's: 'Be the change you want to see in the world.' And it haunted me. I kept going back to that saying. Now standing firm, I'm not prepared to stay silent anymore. I've got other people that need my truth and I will speak. I have never felt as clear as I do now.

If I've had a backlash about speaking out I'm not listening. I'm now 40 years old. I keep hearing people blaming and when people blame they disempower themselves. They give away their personal responsibility and that's why they don't see an answer to their miseries. I used to blame. When I stopped blaming it was like the curtains were pulled back and I thought, 'Oh, there's a world out there!' You've got to make life say, 'Yes' instead of 'No'. I've done that by believing in myself. I had to learn to love me. Pacific Island people often think they don't deserve to be successful. I deserve it and I made it happen. I went and opened doors for me. I took every opportunity that came my way.

I would like to lift up my specific people and culture by challenging them to admit there are problems that need to be dealt with. I will speak out on what I see. This is my story and yeah sure I'm Samoan, but these are societal issues as well. Abuse happens in all cultures. I'd love to see this country stand up tall and hold our hands together as different nationalities and make it work. I figure there's 3.9 million people. It's achievable!

I'm now thankful I went through what I did because it's brought me to a place where I can share my truth. It was necessary for my spiritual side. By sharing my upbringing, my hardship, my pain, I'm finding pleasure because it's encouraging others to say, 'Hey, if she can do it, I can do it too!' It's the power of decision making. We're all born with the tools to be successful. It's knowing how to use those tools and I guess that's what I'm discovering, so I can encourage others.

It's taken this long to find my purpose. My mission is to share my life story. If sharing my truth improves life for women and children in this country then my stance of zero tolerance to abuse is worth it. We all deserve to feel safe and to live happily. I want to encourage other people to see that they too have choices, to plant the seed of change. If the old ways that they've been living are not working, be open to try another way. There's a saying, 'If you always do what you've always done, you'll always get the same result.' I look at my life now with an attitude of gratitude. I'm really thankful for who I am, how I've survived and come through and where I'm going. I'm a lot happier with me.

Soala's message

My message is for people to love and respect themselves — to be responsible and accountable. Because if you do it just filters out to society and people grab on to it. Find your dream! Work out a map of where you want to go in life. Break it down from ten years to five years, to daily. That way you really move forward, just by goal setting and being committed to it. Hop in the river of life and paddle for it. It's worth it! If there is a block find a different way. Don't just turn around and go back. Fear overcomes you if you give up. It's very powerful if you go through fear. If you've lost your dream ignite it again. What did you aspire to as a child? Where did your dream go? Get it back! Write it down! Really see it! You might think, 'Oh, it just got filed away.' That's really where our dreams are. We're all born with a purpose. Sometimes it just gets locked away and we need to find it again. To all women, be strong. You deserve to live your dream.

ENJOYING
THE REWARDS

The power to create quality of life is within us – in our ability to develop and use our own inner compass so that we can act with integrity in the moment of choice . . .

First Things First, Stephen Covey, A. Roger Merrill & Rebecca R. Merrill

When we follow our heart's calling and involve ourselves in the things that truly engage our interest and fire our passion, our life unfolds in wonderful ways. Our dreams often require us to draw on reserves of creativity and perseverance, so they bring out the very best in us. When we do that which we love and continue to give of our best, we can expect to achieve great things. As we expand our knowledge, skills and courage to meet the challenge we experience the exhilaration and freedom of seeing the world from a different perspective and discover we are capable of more than we ever dared to dream.

The endeavours that attract, inspire and excite us reflect our true calling. In pursuing our dreams we express who we really are — our own unique blend of desires, skills, talents and passion. We honour ourselves, and as we do we grow and develop even more. Rewards are found not only in the achievement of dreams, but in the pursuit. There is pleasure in engaging with life in a wholehearted way. Even if we choose to change direction, or our dreams do not evolve as we hoped, we have the satisfaction of knowing we cared enough and had enough courage to 'give it a go'.

Most of us seek meaning in our life. It's important to know our existence on the planet has contributed in some way to the lives of others. Our dreams often provide us with the means to become part of something greater than ourselves, and this can be especially rewarding.

The sense of deep satisfaction that comes with true success is achieved by honourable means. When we live our life with integrity we stand strong in principles and values which uplift humankind: honesty, respect, kindness, compassion, humility and generosity. Life presents us with constant opportunities to choose for or against integrity. Will we achieve our dream by taking the path of honour and generosity or meanness and selfishness? Will we empower others or see them as competition and attempt to diminish them? Will we choose honesty in our dealings with people or will we be so intent on achieving the end result we won't care how we get there? Will we look down on someone because they are different from us? Will we delight in others' success? Will we earn people's love and respect through our considerate, kind actions? Will we forgive someone who has hurt us and reach out to heal the hurt we cause?

The choices we make on a day-to-day basis have a direct impact, not only on our ability to achieve our dreams, but the degree of fulfilment we feel when they are realised. By acting in accordance with our values and principles we are strengthened. When we are true to our self and lead a life we feel good about we create a solid foundation for success. Our conscience is clear and we know in our heart we are deserving of the many blessings in our life.

Lois Muir's commitment to wholeheartedly follow her passion while acting in accordance with her personal philosophies, values and principles has earned her the respect of many people and brought her a huge amount of satisfaction and enjoyment.

Lois Muir

'All of us are only bound by limits of our own imaginations. We set the limits for ourselves.'

Lois is a much-loved and highly respected woman in the world of netball, in which she has been involved for fifty years. She is well known for her talent for creating stable teams connected by what she calls 'an invisible thread' of mutual caring and support. Lois was the coach of the Silver Ferns National Netball Team for fifteen years (1974–1988). During this time her team suffered only nine losses in 102 tests, a testimony to Lois' ability to inspire, motivate and bring out the best in her players.

Her enormous dedication to and passion for netball is reflected in the huge amount of unpaid time Lois has given to the sport. Lois has been a New Zealand representative netballer and basketballer, a qualified umpire, an Otago, then New Zealand netball selector and coach, a member of the Netball Association executive, a member of the Otago Sports Trust and a governor and executive board member of the Sports Foundation – all in a voluntary capacity. Lois would be the first to say she's done it because she's enjoyed it. Her commitment, longevity and success earned her an OBE in 1984. In 1989 Lois had her first paid position in netball, as director of coaching for Netball New Zealand, a position she held for eight years. Lois currently coaches the Wellington netball team, the Capital Shakers. She has three adult sons and lives with her husband Murray Muir in Dunedin.

Passion for me is seeing people enjoying the things they do and growing and succeeding – to see young people improving and believing in themselves. That gives me a great buzz. In my coaching the reward for me has not been winning a World Championship, although I've been coach of a team that's won two of these. The reward has been seeing those young women go on in their lives afterwards and become women in their own right with minds of their own, who are competing and finding themselves and are prepared to stand up and be counted. That, to me, is exciting. I think sport can give confidence to people and that's a marvellous thing.

My passion in sports was really an accident in a way. When I was 9, my father died. I had an older brother and sister and we were great mates, but we were rural people living in Mataura, in Southland. My mother never drove a car, so if I wanted to go to netball training I had to ride a bike a mile to catch a train, then travel eight miles on the train. Basketball training was even further. But that was what I had to do if I wanted to go, so it made me independent.

I think losing my father made me appreciate life a little more. It made me do things today rather than waiting, I don't mean by being totally reckless, but I learned to look ahead and take the opportunities that came. Coming from a rural background you realise there are opportunities there but you've got to work a bit harder to be seen. Nothing's laid on for you.

My mother wanted me to learn the piano, but that wasn't high in my priorities. We had a lovely piano, but it really wasn't for me. I was always rushing to the music teacher and trying to fudge not having practised. My older sister came back from Teachers College when I was still in primary school. She played in basketball and netball teams and her teams were always short, so because I was tall for my age she bullied Mum into letting me fill in. It was quite funny. I used to bike down the road and sneak on a little bit of lipstick and try and look older and play. I loved playing and became obsessed with the game.

We moved to Dunedin in about 1950. I was 15 and I went to Otago Girls for about eight weeks, then an opportunity came up at a pharmacy to learn how to manage the business. The woman pharmacist, Mrs Peggy Cameron, was a great influence in my life at that stage. She was a woman who had come from a rural area, left school with only a Higher Leaving Certificate, married a pharmacist and then gone back to school to get educated. She got her University Entrance and studied and became a pharmacist, one of the early women in New Zealand to get that qualification. And so she showed me that anything was possible. I was going to go back for more education as well, but I didn't. I got too wound up with my sport.

In those days I was doing thousands of things – playing or training every night of the week except Friday nights when I worked till nine. I wanted to make the New Zealand netball team so every lunch hour I'd grab a sandwich and go to the gym down the road and do some training. Mrs Cameron used to say that I always had indigestion, but I'd take something for that, gulp it down and back to work. It was fitting my netball into my life really. It was enjoyable!

Enjoyment is a key word for me. I'm a person who enjoys life and is always looking forward. I like to plan well because I believe nothing ever happens by accident. I'm not a perfectionist because I think that's over the top, but I'm a little driven because I think you only come by this way once. I'm here now and I want to enjoy it and it's what you make of it. I think when you're always looking forward there are always challenges ahead. I believe we take our imagination with us and that helps to set the challenges for us. All of us are only bound by limits of our own imaginations. We set the limits for ourselves. I see that in young people all the time and that's why I love coaching.

The coach can only give the player the confidence to discover themselves. If someone is playing a pretty ordinary game and I suggest a couple of things to her and she works on it and she becomes more successful, she's really now master of her own destiny, because she sees she can do it and the little bit of advice has helped. So all I'm doing is planting the seeds, showing her that if she thought a little bit more into it, how much better she could be. To me the exciting thing has been that as you empower people, you have to be better because they're a challenge to you. That's the fun in coaching really. That's why I will never hold back any knowledge from anyone.

When I'm coaching I'm often pushing people a little bit beyond where they've had their own horizon, just helping them to lift their horizon a little bit more. People often limit themselves. If I say, 'You've played quite well today, but there are things you can improve on, which we know about', we are moving forward. But if I say, 'You played well', and you say, 'No, no, I didn't', you've got only the negative thoughts you're putting out. I often think as women we don't accept praise well. I've had women I've worked with and they've played well and I've said that and they say, 'Oh no, I did this wrong and I did that wrong.' Learning to accept praise is so important.

I think success is in the mind of the individual. A lot of people think the score on the scoreboard at the end of the game is success, whereas I don't look at it like that. I believe it's the measure you set yourself. I think with very little thought and effort we can do things better. I can achieve something but I'm always saying, 'How can it be different?' Even when a team is playing well and it's quite successful you're always evaluating what you're doing. I enjoy that because I think it stops you from becoming complacent. If you want to be Number One you don't say, 'Aren't we good?', you say, 'We can do better.'

Coaching can be a difficult job. I've always believed in doing the simple things well and that's stood me in good stead. I think you've got to have respect. I can have a laugh with people, but when I'm away with New Zealand teams representing our country I'm a reasonably hard taskmaster because I'm looking for the end result all the time. At World Championships you really have to be a little bit distant from the players because at the end of the day you have to put the finger on them when decisions have to be made. They have to respect that you're making the best decision for the total group's end results. I think when they believe you're doing that you have earned their respect.

Conflict is only conflict because there's not understanding of both sides of the story. I think when everyone knows they are of value you don't have so much conflict in a group. Conflict happens when your view is the only one you want to put across and they have got another view and that's the only one they want put across. Each of us has got good points so if we put them together and see what we can pull out of it we're both going to be stronger.

All the early years I was involved with netball we were in the voluntary era so I never got paid, but I didn't mind because it was exciting. When the opportunity came up for me to coach my boys were very young but my husband Murray said to me, 'If you don't do it now, when you're ready to do it they may not want you. We'll worry about the details later.' He was a sportsperson in his own right so he was supportive. Murray earned a salary and I spent it faster than he could earn it. We employed a Karitane Nurse to help with the boys when I went away for the first three tours. So my children grew up with me spending money and going away. It taught them that each of us has got a right to a life of our own and I always wanted them to know that.

People have helped me along the way – I would never have got there without their support. I had a marvellous group of supportive women here in Dunedin. When my children were little and I was busy coaching they were looking after my kids. They are the people I still remember. I think it's so important not to forget our roots.

I coached New Zealand teams for seventeen years. It totally absorbed me for all that time and I loved every minute of it, then when we won the World Championship in Glasgow in 1987 about three top players were going to retire. Every other time I was looking forward to that challenge and just for one moment at the end of the World Championship I thought, 'There's a bit of work here', and I knew I shouldn't be there. I felt that the next World Championship should have someone younger and fresher than me on the sideline. It was time for me to move on to other things.

The discovery that I had breast cancer in 1998 was one of those things called a hiccup. My mother and sister have both had it but I'd never dwelt on the possibility I'd get it, so I got a bit of a surprise. I went for an ordinary mammogram and I was going away to coach the Wellington team for the National championships later that week, so they did an ultrasound and biopsy straightaway. My doctor rang me the next day and said, 'Yes, it is positive.' So I said to him, 'Well rightoh, what's the plan? Do you know a good surgeon?'

I went to Wellington on Saturday and I told them I had to go home on Monday because one of my sons had to go to see a specialist. So I flew back to Dunedin, saw the surgeon and made the hospital appointment then I flew back to Wellington that night and finished off the netball practice, because we were going to Hamilton to the National championships the next day.

I stayed the week in Hamilton and never told anyone until after the championship. Then when we did the debrief after the last game I said to the girls, 'Well, I've got a bit of a hiccup. I've got breast cancer and I'm going into hospital on Wednesday. Why I'm telling you guys is because I've got a game plan and I'm going to stick to it better than some of you have stuck to our game plan this week.' Some of them were pretty upset so I said, 'Look, you're young women, it may happen to you sometime later in your life. I've got a family background of it and I'm going forward. Netball is a hot gossipy place. Things go round the country like bush telegraph. You're my disciples. You can say I'm handling it well and that it's all under control.' I think it's how you handle it that makes the difference. And knowing they were supporting me helped too.

Then I went round some of my old mates and let them know, because what happens when you're sick and you haven't told people is they don't know if you want to talk about it or not. They're thinking that you're not looking well and they don't want to say anything. They might even cross the street so they don't have to talk to you because they don't know how to handle it and they think they might shed a tear. So it's actually much better to have it out in the open.

Having breast cancer didn't change my attitude to life. I've always believed life is what we make it and something is going to catch up with us one day. We never know what. I was certainly enthusiastic to support the breast cancer appeal, but I didn't want to appear as a person out there playing the violins about it because that's not me. It's going forward that's important and I felt I wanted to get that message across.

A lot of things in my life have just evolved and I've loved the challenges. I've taken opportunities as they've come along. I think we often say we'll do something tomorrow, but you know it's the people who make the effort to do it today who really get things done. I believe in not looking back too far over your shoulder and not dwelling on things. You're always looking out of your body so you're only as old as you feel. That's the fun of it really! It's taking myself outside my comfort zone all the time. Just a little bit, just a nudge out of it. It just keeps life more interesting, without going overboard.

Lois' message

I've always said we are masters of our own destiny, because it is the effort we put in that gives the results. Enjoyment is very important so find something you enjoy and give it a little bit more thought and effort and you can be very good at it. I think even when we went to school there were subjects we liked and subjects we didn't like. The ones we enjoyed we did well at. It's exactly the same thing in life. It's building on those things we enjoy. The opportunities are there but you've got to take them. We create more opportunities than we ever find. Sometimes people are looking for opportunities, but you've got to generate them. They don't just pop out, you've got to make them yourself. I think it's important to always be looking forward and lifting your horizon just another little notch.

COUNTING AND SHARING BLESSINGS

If every one of our lives is to be worth living it will be because
we have allowed ourselves to discover the radiant power and
ease, magic and beauty of generosity.

Forgiveness and Other Acts of Love, Stephanie Dowrick

Each of us has much to be grateful for, yet it is easy to forget this. We can get so caught up in all that we have to do, we overlook our great good fortune in having the ability to do so much. Regardless of our circumstances, the fulfilment we feel is a direct reflection of our ability to count our blessings. Gratitude is a state of awareness – a way of looking at the world with appreciation and acknowledging all that we have. The practice of gratitude opens our eyes and hearts to the many pleasures we might otherwise take for granted: seeing our loved one's smile, snuggling into a warm bed, listening to good music, eating a nourishing meal or sharing a pleasant hour with a friend. Appreciation lifts our spirits and transforms the mundane to the delightful.

We can choose to focus on what we don't have or what we do have; the half-empty or the half-full cup. We can indulge ourselves in indifference, complaints or criticisms or give thanks for all that is going well. If we are prone to focusing on what we consider 'wrong' in our life we can break this self-defeating habit by choosing, moment to moment, to see the abundance in our life rather than the lack. Some people find having a gratitude book to record blissful moments, happy memories and others' kind words helps to develop a stronger appreciation of the good things in their life.

Gratitude paves the way to our dreams. Appreciation creates the confidence, optimism and joy we need to sustain ourselves. The more we acknowledge and embrace the good in our life the more we open up to the many opportunities all around us. As we count our blessings we create or strengthen a belief in an abundant world where it is possible to achieve success in our endeavours. We are empowered to continue to move purposefully towards our dreams. Our life is richer and we feel more fulfilled.

Giving is an integral part of achievement. Through giving we acknowledge the abundance of our life and our interconnectedness with others. It doesn't matter who we are or how much money we have, we can make a difference by sharing the many blessings in our lives. Rather than clutching our resources to ourselves, afraid we have insufficient time, money or energy to give, we can choose to be generous and share with an open heart, having faith that our needs will be taken care of.

We each have the power to uplift those we come into contact with by the friendly, appreciative, honouring way we interact with them. Many acts of generosity cost nothing: our smile, attention, kind and encouraging words, affection, appreciation and helpful gestures – yet these gifts mean much to the people we encounter.

There are countless ways we can share our blessings including: listening to someone in need; showing tolerance and patience towards someone slower or less competent than ourselves; offering a helping hand; giving time, energy and money to good causes; taking the time to chat with a lonely person; expressing concern at anothers' disappointment or loss; surprising someone with a gift or card; offering praise, encouragement or enthusiasm or doing voluntary work for a community group. We can also uplift another by having the grace to accept their offer of help so they too can experience the pleasure of giving.

Our acts of kindness can make an enormous difference. Day-to-day life is a challenge for many. If we look around we will see people who need our kindness. Our society has many people struggling against the odds, many causes begging to be taken up and many needs waiting to be filled. We can't save the world but we can acknowledge those who are worse off than ourselves and reach out and do what we can to help, even in small ways.

The most profound gift we can give is to acknowledge other people's struggles, to care that they hurt, to reach out with compassion and to strive to make our little corner of the world a better place. That act of love makes our growth and achievements truly worthwhile. In these final stories Hinewehi Mohi and Lucy Lawless count their blessings and talk about how they share them with others. The ways in which their appreciation and generosity enhance their own lives, as well as those around them, are very apparent.

Hinewehi Mohi

'If I can inspire just one person to do something more with their life through my music then I will die a happy person.'

Hinewehi is a singer and songwriter who expresses her passion, love and Maori heritage through her music. She grew up on a farm in Hawke's Bay and when she was 13, she went away to board at St Joseph's Maori Girls' College. It was there, in the choir, that she developed her beautiful singing voice. As a young woman Hinewehi studied for a BA in Maori Studies at Waikato University and was positively influenced by many Maori lecturers and fellow students there.

Hinewehi became the producer of TVNZ's Marae *television programme in 1995, and continued in that role until her daughter, Hineraukatauri, was born with cerebral palsy four years ago. Her hauntingly beautiful album,* Oceania, *was produced in collaboration with friend and musician Jaz Coleman in 1999. It features a blend of traditional and contemporary Maori music and is a celebration of her daughter's strength of spirit. It is also a celebration of the Maori language and culture that means so much to Hinewehi.*

I feel like I was nothing until my daughter Hineraukatauri was born. All the trivialities that came and went in my life just seem sort of silly now. Of course I wouldn't say the people I've come in contact with and the experiences I've had haven't been interesting and exciting and haven't taught me things, but absolutely nothing compares to the last four years of my life since my daughter was born with cerebral palsy. I've gone from the complete turmoil of not knowing if she was going to survive to the absolute joy and celebration of her response to music or pictures or people she's become familiar with.

She inspires me every day because she is able to battle on and still rise above all the restrictions of her condition. She can't even breathe on her own. She has a tracheotomy tube, so that's a huge restriction. The medical concern and anxiety I feel when she's sick is very draining. And she has this wonderful character. She makes the most of every wonderful thing in her life. Whether it be the sensation of having a bath or something about a book she's enjoying or music she is listening to, she'll absolutely maximise that enjoyment and express to everyone around her how cool it is. She's an incredible delight in my life.

I guess I have some kind of strength that's come from somewhere in order to be able to cope with Hineraukatauri's special needs. Before she was born I was a producer for Television New Zealand but this is the biggest production ever. It has changed over the years as her physical strength has improved. I don't think things are any easier but they've definitely become more manageable because I've worked out systems. I guess all my character comes out in the way I care for her because she pushes those characteristics to their absolute fullest because of her needs. Deep down I'm a bit of a marshmallow, but I try to be seen as someone who's coping all the time. There have been many times when I've felt like I haven't coped very well, but for my daughter I've had to do my best.

The extremes are just incredible. It's been a roller coaster; less so now because I think that if anything was to happen to her we've shared so much together anyway – the extremes of what life presents, but in a more compact time. I do feel constantly tired, but I think that's a state of motherhood that you just take onboard.

Within a year of my daughter's birth, my relationship with her father ended. I was a solo mother and I didn't really have time for myself so I didn't really have time to grieve for the loss of her true life potential until a couple of years after she was born, and even then it was with difficulty, because she still demands so much time.

When I found myself alone with my daughter I thought it would be a solo gig. I'd really resigned myself to the fact I would just have to endure this on my own because it just seemed too huge for anyone to take on. That was really quite frightening so I didn't dwell on it too long. If someone had said to me two years ago that I was going to marry a wonderful man I would have said, 'Oh yeah, right!' But I have and it's all come together very quickly.

When I met George I couldn't believe someone could be as unfazed by my daughter as he has been. It has been really hard for a lot of people close to us to know how to deal with the fact that my daughter is unable to interact and participate in the world as much as we'd all hoped, so people's involvement with her is at varying levels. But as soon as George met Hineraukatauri he wanted to hold her and make contact. I was immediately charmed by that. So aside from loving him for myself, I love him for how he loves my daughter.

Before my daughter was born my lifestyle was very involved in kaupapa Maori things, with initiatives that were a special sort of role modeling focus for young Maori people. Aotearoa was very much at my fingertips. I was out and about and travelling around New Zealand all the time. Now I'm very isolated from that world because I can't get out and even taking my daughter to hui is just too difficult. So that side of my commitment to Maori things has been curbed, which is why it's so wonderful I can sing, because I can still reach out with my music. Music is wonderful for that. Even if the language isn't fully understood the sentiment is felt through the music.

Until my daughter was born I always did music as a sideline and then I had to put my television career on hold. I could have just wasted the last four years in terms of my music but I've been lucky that I've had opportunities open to me and I've been open to those opportunities and I've gone with the flow. Essentially my music has come to the fore because I've been encouraged by the producer of *Oceania* to use it to grieve. You know sometimes if you're in pain and feel like you're withering away, you just want to go to the top of a mountain and scream. To a certain extent I've been able to just really push my vocal limitations to the fullest – the absolute maximum – and that has helped me to heal.

And the glossy, fluffy side of the music industry gives me a bit of pampering because I get made up for my shows. I can actually have a little bit of time out while I'm transformed from slopping around in my slippers to this kind of diva pop star, so it's a bit like play-acting – like dress ups. I really enjoy performing and I know I have a special talent in this area. I'd hate to go through life without fully utilising those skills and sharing my gift with people. If I can inspire just one person to do something more with their life through my music then I will die a happy person. So I guess that's what I need to appreciate, that I do have a gift I can share and if anyone benefits from it then I'm really lucky. I just really love to sing and to share that part of me and it's empowering for me to express the femininity of my Maori culture. I hope that all cultures and ages can relate to it or appreciate it or want to just be cruising to it.

When I sang the national anthem in Maori at the Rugby World Cup in 1999 there was a huge protest. I was so upset at that time. We were in England promoting our music and I was feeling like a bit of a lonely diplomat trying to promote the culture positively. It was great when I was asked to sing at the World Cup. I thought, 'This is something that makes every New Zealander feel warm fuzzies.' Because even if you're not into rugby there's that national pride that comes through, especially for something we excel at.

Our band performed at Twickenham before the game and as soon as everyone saw the piupiu on the haka boys they just erupted with enthusiasm and excitement for what was going to happen. We performed and it was just so well received. It was like we were rock stars. It was exhilarating! I felt really proud that we could portray this very positive, energised, vibrant aspect of the culture. Then when I sang the anthem, it was a natural thing for me to sing it in Maori.

I was totally blown away when Paul Holmes rang me and said, 'Wow, it's going crazy here with people very angry about the singing of the anthem in Maori.' He was really supportive. That was the first I knew. Those initial few weeks were all very negative and I was scared to come home but when I did it was fine and I've just been so overwhelmed with the positive support. I knew Maori would be excited about the language of this land being sung in the way it was, but Pakeha people have also said to me that they thought it was wonderful and they felt it was as much a part of them as anyone in this country. That made me feel really glad – relieved – that things weren't as bad as I had initially thought.

Even so it was a process I didn't really need. It was a difficult time and it created so much turmoil. Just coping with my daughter and getting through each day is quite big, so if I get anything on top of that it chips away at my energy and positivity then I just find it really difficult to bear. Perhaps when I was a little bit younger and feistier I could have taken things on a little more forcefully. I know what my convictions are in terms of Maori issues, but I don't see the point in trying to turn around the thinking of someone who blatantly doesn't want to understand any culture other than their own. I've never really been a confrontational person but I just like to show a positive and pro-Maori side to the way I feel and the way I think Aotearoa should be reflected. It's certainly not anti-Pakeha, I never want to exclude anyone.

I don't know if I achieved much but I feel glad that it's at least brought those ideas to people's attention. I think we try to pretend that we're understanding of all cultures in this country but there are many underlying feelings of bigotry and misunderstanding about Maori issues in particular. It just highlighted to me that there were a lot of prejudices that perhaps had been laying a little bit dormant and it just took something like that to explode it again. One positive thing that's come out of it though is that a directive has come from government saying that both Maori and English should be sung as the national anthem.

I feel very lucky with my life. The love and support I've felt since my daughter's birth has been very overwhelming – enough to last me a lifetime. So I feed on those experiences when I'm feeling a little less energised by talking about them with friends or just thinking about them. That's incredibly uplifting! When Bubba was just 3 months old we had a fundraiser concert to help pay for her treatment and all my muso friends sang for her. The love in that venue was just profound. It kept me flying high for days. George and I are constantly amazed by people's love and support. It was heightened when we were organising our wedding. People's generosity and goodwill really inspired us to think that we could do anything.

I feel very happy now in my relationship with my husband and that sets the basis for my relationship with my daughter and family and friends. I think I've probably been looking for him all my life. I have really incredible support systems around me. I have caregivers who are paid to help with my daughter's care but I also rely on friendships. I have wonderful friends and I feel terribly beholden to them for the love they give me constantly and the ways they boost me when I'm feeling tired. Even though they have busy lives themselves they still take the time to ring me or see me or provide some other sort of support.

I guess it's interesting that a crisis situation brings out different characteristics in those around you. Some of my friends I didn't see for a few years after my daughter was born simply because they felt they couldn't cope with seeing my situation as it was. And I don't judge them as being any worse as friends than before that happened. I just really relied on the close and supportive friendships I did have.

I know too that you have to work at friendships and I sometimes feel like I don't give enough back. I can't necessarily keep contact on a physical level, but I always try to maintain contact over the phone and with e-mail and postcards when we travel, so I can just show people I still care and love them even though I'm just not able to spare the time away from my commitments.

I've always tried to be happy so that's probably something that's pulled me through some of the harder things I've had to tackle, particularly in recent years. I've never been afraid of hard work either, coming from family that has always had to work hard for everything. Nothing was handed to us on a platter.

I grew up on a farm in a small rural district in Hawke's Bay. It was a charmed existence. I was lucky that I didn't have anything tumultuous around me until my teens when my parents split up. I was sheltered from anything that could have been detrimental to my emotional development. I was just really lucky and given every encouragement to follow the pursuits I took up. I had so much freedom and space and fresh air and the luxury of animals in my life.

My childhood taught me about being positive I guess and all the reasons why we should be happy. It sort of sounds cheesy, but it's a really basic life principle to be happy, isn't it? And yet it's so elusive for some people. They never are in a situation where finding happiness is an easy thing. I've always had choices in my life and I think that's something which has taught me it is possible to be in the state of contentedness, innocence and naivety my childhood represented.

I guess that even when things have been really difficult for me I've always known I could be happy. Even if things were tough at the time there was a light at the end of the tunnel. I think when people have had a difficult upbringing that can be very hard to rise above. It takes incredible character to be able to overcome childhood abuse. I'm inspired by people who rise above adversity and are still incredible leaders or do wonderful things within the community and take on those leadership roles, particularly for Maori because there's that extra burden of expectation and stereotypes that makes the job so much more difficult.

I have a very personal relationship with God and a very intimate one and I don't usually share that with anyone. That relationship has fluctuated over the years but I don't think its intensity has lessened. I've had a gentle sort of respect and appreciation for my faith. I think it's probably similar to my grandmother's. She's funny. She doesn't go to church often but she has this wonderful regime of prayer. I just see her lips moving with her eyes closed and I know she's grounding herself and just having a bit of time out with herself — working through another spiritual plane. I think that's really cool!

I always feel really calm after I pray and even if things don't go exactly how I want I still feel I've made a real connection. I don't really analyse whether or not my prayers have been answered. I just feel good that I've had this connection with God. That way I don't feel like I've been let down or denied or I've expected too much. There's no judgments. It's very much a therapeutic working-through so that my head gets around the problem. I do get worried that I tend to really pray when Hineraukatauri is sick. I sometimes think, 'Gosh I shouldn't just wait for the desperado times and get all spiritually inclined.'

I'm quite a practical person. Although I have this spiritual base to my life I don't really think, 'Why me?' Because why not me? I get a little bit frustrated when people say everything happens for a reason. Then I think, 'OK, what was the reason for this happening to Hineraukatauri and what's the reason for starvation in Ethiopia?' I don't simplify things that happen in my life that easily, but I don't beat myself up about what might have been either.

There's just no point in feeling sorry for myself for too long. I'm always trying to look for the positive. Hineraukatauri can just turn my whole day around by smiling. I feel very blessed. I'm not trying to sound like a martyr and saying, 'Yeah that's my lot and I wouldn't have it any other way,' because of course I would love her to be doing things that other four-year-olds are doing. But I do feel I'm a really lucky person.

My primary focus is my family and making sure that we can be happy and content. We have very simple needs really. Just a bit of peace and quiet and time for ourselves but that's still difficult to achieve at times. I feel that I'm in a position with my music to make people aware of children with special needs and people with differences and I'm really committed to that. I think it's really important that Hineraukatauri be given the opportunity to do her job too, which is to inspire people and to teach them a little bit more about themselves and to be more open and understanding of others.

Hinewehi's message

I think first finding what you're best at and then allowing a little to chance and a little to your drive will eventually help you achieve your goals. The most important thing is to identify your skills and your gifts and to work on those. Sometimes people expend too much energy hoping they'll be able to achieve in a certain area that isn't necessarily an area of expertise. It's about being honest with yourself. I've seen some people try too hard. Some people are very ambitious and able to push through but sometimes they're misunderstood because they're actually not channelling their true talent. They're not feeling fulfilled and not achieving to the heights they want to because they haven't actually isolated out what they're best at. If they are working at something that isn't necessarily their absolute strength they may face a lot of knock-backs. It's finding and developing that area of real passion.

Lucy Lawless

'I believe as human beings our potential is unlimited, especially if we see it that way.'

Lucy is the famous star of the internationally successful television series Xena: Warrior Princess *which screens in more than 115 countries. Despite her phenomenal success Lucy remains delightfully natural, down-to-earth and friendly.*

She was born in Auckland, in 1968, into a large Catholic family of seven children. Her father was the mayor of Mount Albert. In her role as mayoress, her mother organised entertainment for senior citizens, giving Lucy her first taste of performing, and when she was 10 Lucy decided she wanted to be an actor.

After a brief stint in the gold fields, Lucy was married, in 1988, in the Australian outback. Her daughter Daisy was born the same year. The family moved to Vancouver to enable Lucy to attend an acting school there for a year. Although the marriage broke up soon after, Lucy and her ex-husband remain friends.

In 1998 Lucy married Rob Tapert, the executive producer of Xena *and in 1999 she gave birth to a son, Julius. Very aware of childrens' vulnerability, Lucy became distressed about the issue of child abuse so prevalent in our society. Wanting to find proactive solutions, Lucy helped to found the Safe and Sound action group in September 2000 to increase public awareness and raise funds to address this issue. It has been announced that the sixth series of* Xena *is to be the final one. Lucy is looking forward to spending more time with her family and would like to have more children. She also intends to pursue a movie career.*

I always knew I wanted to act and never seriously entertained any other career. I can remember as a child singing and dancing to my records and tucking scarves into my knickers and being a ballerina, even though I was derided fiercely for it by my brothers. I did a lot of plays and musicals all through school and that was great. I remember in Standard Three being asked, 'What do you want to be?' and me secretly thinking, 'I really want to be an actress', but I always knew that in New Zealand you have to be a quiet achiever. If you blurt it out you're going to get hammered.

I always believed in my potential to achieve what I wanted. When I read the old diary I wrote in those first seven years of my career, I see I was very torn. I knew my destination, I just didn't know how to get there. But I always kept on compass and believed I would make it.

I'm passionate about my work. I just thrive on it. I love my colleagues and the pursuit of excellence and I really expect excellence. I don't see any reason for anybody to be giving less than the best they have that day. None of us are 100 per cent all of the time but nobody on our crew is allowed to be repeatedly sloppy. Now that I'm one of the more senior people – not only one of the longest-serving, I'm also one of the oldest around – I expect that of others because if you don't demand excellence from people they'll never excel. It has been demanded of me that I be a hard worker and always try to be a good example.

In my work I owe a lot to a guy called Donny Duncan, who was our Director of Photography. At the beginning of *Xena* I was full of myself and there was so much clamour of my own ego and excitement about the world. So much ringing in my own head that I couldn't hear or see anybody else's efforts or the demands of their jobs. And part of the job of the lead actor in a series is to let other people work on you and you have to let them light, stand there while they put make-up on and just fiddle with you. That's quite difficult to get used to but I eventually realised their job is also my job. One day Donny turned around and told me in no uncertain terms to pull my socks up – to just stand there and cooperate. That was a lesson I'll never forget. It gave me a really great key to happiness in my working life – to appreciate other people's input and brilliance and their work ethic. The people I work with are actually my strength, so I treat them well.

It's an unusual lifestyle when we're filming. I'm told where I have to be, what I'm having for lunch that day, what time to get up and what time I'm going home. I don't even have to think about what I'll wear because I get up in the morning, in the dark more than likely, and put on a cruddy old T-shirt or something. Nobody is going to see me and my clothes are going to get ruined by the filthy brown body make-up they put on me every day. It's a pretty simple life. That took a long time to adjust to – a couple of years to surrender completely.

In the fourth season of *Xena* I had a real crisis of faith. I couldn't stand it anymore. I felt so constricted and constrained in every way and work was unrelenting, extremely physical. My co-star Renee had been written out for a few episodes so it was all on me. We were filming down at the base of Mt Ruapehu, on the Desert Road, and it was bitterly cold. The crew loves going on location. They get to wear all these warm clothes, while I'm wearing this chammy. I'm freezing – working twelve to fourteen hour days and having to be the morale leader. The local girls were amazing – uncomplaining, hardy, fabulous – but a lot of the Auckland girls were brats. If they see me misbehave they think that's how it's done so I've learnt not to have paddies in front of new people. So I had to be sure not to spit the dummy, because there was no way out. It was awful! I'd be lying on the ground freezing and I'd cry, I'd just revert to feeling 8 years old and I'd say my Hail Marys to get me through. I just revert to that mantra – this too shall pass – that's so ingrained in me. That's what I know from my Catholic upbringing and in times of stress that's where I go.

That was a really low time. I didn't know where I was going next, but I needed some skills to go somewhere different. Nothing I'd learnt was helping me anymore. I was stuck. I had everything – a wonderful boyfriend and daughter, a great career, a wonderful house. Why wasn't I happy? I knew it wasn't external. There was nothing I could blame. It was within me.

During that time I did Anthony Robbins' self-help tapes. Those tapes really did help me sort myself out. Anthony Robbins gave you questions to ask yourself to help you sort out what you really wanted in life. He doesn't tell you what to think, he teaches you how to think.

You've got to realise what you fear and deal with that. I did one tape every day and I did all the exercises and I didn't rush them and that gave me new skills.

Most of all I wanted to be happy and I knew I would not be happy as an old woman without children. I knew that one day I'd wake up and find myself 80 years old, that there will be an end to my life and what I really wanted to be was happy and mobile. Happiness for me means to be surrounded by youth and laughter and that meant I had to have a family. Equally I knew I would not be a happy woman if I was not able to work. I wanted to carry on working because I love it. I don't love the destination, I love the journey of working. I love every day going to work. So I realised that part of the problem was the fear of balancing family and work.

There are very few women I consider role models in this industry, particularly in Hollywood. The biggest challenge in my chosen career is the fact that as I get older there's always going to be someone younger, prettier and newer coming through. It's a world that craves youth and my challenge is never to bow to that. The actress Susan Sarandon is someone I admire. She has said, 'I don't have to play the Hollywood game to have a career – to not have children and preserve my breasts and my stomach and God knows what.' She's got three children and even though she didn't work for a lot of years she now picks and chooses her work. Her talent and her beauty and her intelligence have preserved her career. I'd describe Susan Sarandon as loving, worthy, funny and definitely sexy – a fully integrated human being.

I do have far more options at this stage of my career because I can generate my own work. I'm not waiting for somebody else to hand me a work opportunity on a silver platter. I will go and make it happen like my mum and dad did.

My dad came from nothing. His mother died soon after he was born, probably of despair. She got septicemia and left eight sons – two sets of twins – my dad was the youngest. By the time he was 15 his father died of lung cancer, a long, miserable death. So the kids were raised by Catholic nuns and a maiden aunt. Dad went on to become the mayor of Mount Albert. That taught me you don't have to come from somewhere to get somewhere. You can just get off your backside and make things happen, so admit no impediment. It's funny the things you learn without even knowing it.

I had a fantastic childhood. It was pretty rough and tumble because I've got a lot of brothers. My mum and dad never said, 'You can't!' We had so much fun when we were kids. Mum would get us up at nine o'clock at night even on a school night and say, 'Let's make some glue and do a collage', and we'd make things out of beans and macaroni. There were always boxes of string and glue and creative stuff around the house. I learned a lot watching my mother, who is an amazingly active woman in the community. I'd put on plays and adapt fairy tales for the old folks' homes with my friend Michele Spijkerbosch. We'd have little concerts at home and do flips off the porch. We did terrifying things really. My poor mother! We must have given her a thousand heart attacks!

I had my dad on a pedestal and it's taken me thirty years to get him off and then I keep sneaking him back up there. His word was really strong and he was particularly influential in empowering me. There were two things that stand out that helped to give me great self-esteem. One was a great belief in the unseen. I grew up very Catholic. When I was 7 or 8 I remember my dad telling me people could bend spoons with their minds or they could move objects if only they could focus enough. That was a shock because that was nowhere in Catholic doctrine as far as I knew. It made a big impression on me, that there was something more to the world than just the Catholic Church and my family.

The other influential thing was I'd always heard that marriage is sacred, yet my father said to me at a very early age, 'If a man hits you, even if he's your husband, you get out of there. Never put up with it.' That was very powerful because I knew that I was worth more than that, and hearing it from my dad was a great thing.

I believe in holding your family dear because they're all we really have at the end of the day. I believe as human beings our potential is unlimited, especially if we see it that way. Stagnation is something I fear, not trying – not risking. Taking calculated risks is important. It's that need to have comfort and security and belonging on one hand, against spontaneity and adventure on the other. I find I can have both but it's a constant, gentle, balancing act.

The beliefs and values I live by are that life is bountiful; the harder you work the luckier you get. Be nice, be professional, be good, be good at what you do, take it pretty seriously, but also you've got to have a lot of laughs. I've learnt if you can't be with the ones you love, love the ones you're with. When my husband is away I'm not miserable because I can't be with him, because I'm with these people now. This is all I've got. I'm careful not to wish my life away. I've realised there are some things I can't change, so I change my attitude to them instead.

Nowadays I make decisions based on my intuition and that really does help me do the right thing. My heart tells me which way to go. It's very black and white really. This way makes me feel sad and uncomfortable, this way makes me feel powerful and good and it makes the world feel right. I don't know if my intuition has got stronger or if I have just learnt to trust it and yield more easily to it. I believe when we use our intuition the sort of people we respect will be attracted to us and will respect us.

Sometimes I'll have my head telling me to do something but if I don't feel that it's right I won't do it. For example someone wanted a credit on the opening shots of the show. They wanted to get their name and their face upfront, and the lawyers were saying, 'Are you crazy? You're the star of the show. You don't share. It's not done.' I was saying, 'This doesn't feel right to me. This person works really hard.' So we did it and it was the right decision. Had I stood in the way of that I think it would have put our friendship on a whole different level. It would have ruined things. So I realise that sometimes I know better than other people do, not only for me but for the show.

I used to feel bad because I wanted everything. It seemed like that might be an unreasonable attitude. Now I know it's not. Most of us fear that if I have a successful job and a nice house then maybe my marriage is going to screw up because I can't have it all. That's just too lucky. Something terrible is going to happen. And then I realised that's just self-sabotage. I've learnt from Nelson Mandela's inauguration speech: 'Who am I to be brilliant, gorgeous, talented, fabulous? Actually who are you not to be? You are a child of God . . .' I decided that was a much better attitude to have. Really the luckier you think you are, the more pleasant you are to people, and the more things do come to you. It seems to be true that the more you give away, the more comes to you.

The other things that are important in life for me are making a contribution to my community so that I feel connected and having a connection to a higher power. I think that's a human need, to be connected to something greater than that we can see and touch. I always consider myself really blessed.

Lucy's message

It's so important to follow your dreams. It is possible to succeed. There's nothing to fear but fear itself. Everybody comes from somewhere. Who was going to pick a little middle-class girl from Mt Albert to be in Hollywood someday? Nelson Mandela was right, the world is a bountiful place. God wants you to have all of those things you want. Don't sabotage one dream for the other.

I believe in tithing and I really recommend it. I guess it counteracts that self-sabotage thing. If you hold something to yourself it's never going to grow. It's never going to proliferate if you don't put it out there. When we give, things come back to us tenfold. That was in the Bible. So just spread the joy. You won't even miss it. You won't miss the money or the time or whatever. It'll feed you. Everything comes back to you.

PERSONAL
REFLECTIONS

As we write, digging ourselves out of denial, our memories, dreams and creative plans all move to the surface. We discover anew that we are creative beings.

The Artist's Way, Julia Cameron

Many useful insights are contained in the pages of this book. For those readers seeking direction or wanting to pursue specific dreams, the questions and exercises on the following pages are designed to help you to go a step further by reflecting on your personal process. Writing is a powerful means of personal growth and self-expression.

PURSUING DREAMS

- If you were doing what you love how would your life be different? What changes would you make?
- Where do your interests and natural talents lie?
- What secret longings do you have that are lying dormant or 'tucked away'?
- In the past what activities have captured your interest and felt most compelling? (This is an indication of your passion at work.)
- If you followed the calling of your passion where would it take you?
- What activities do you most love doing and what energises you?
- Write a 'wish list' of all the activities you would love to do if anything were possible.
- Make a list of the special dreams you hope to achieve.

BELIEVING

- Do you contemplate your dreams wistfully with little hope of achieving them or are you reasonably confident you will succeed?
- Do you believe you deserve to succeed in your endeavours?
- What changes (if any) would you need to make to your current self-image if you were successful in your endeavours?
- Start adopting these changes now by visualising yourself as already there and affirming that you have the attributes you need.
- To develop a more positive self-image, list your major accomplishments to date, then list your positive qualities.
- Write down all the positive things you can ever remember people

telling you about yourself. Continue to add to this list.

- Make a list of all the negative beliefs that stand in the way of your dream by completing the following sentence:

I would like to achieve _____ but

_____.

- Identify the limiting beliefs on your list (as opposed to genuine challenges that need to be overcome) and make a list of positive beliefs that directly counteract the limitations stated on your previous list. Read these new beliefs often.

DISCOVERING YOUR PURPOSE

Your purpose is a reflection of who you really are and what is important to you. It can give you an overall direction to your life and a reference point to consider as you set your goals. To clarify your purpose reflect on the following questions:

- What are you happiest doing?
- What do you care deeply about?
- What are the most important values in your life?
- What is the most significant contribution you would like to make?
- Have you experienced times when you were totally absorbed in working on a project for hours without feeling tired? What kind of a project was this?
- Make a list of the times in your life when you felt deeply satisfied because what you were doing was important to you.
- What is the common denominator between those times on your list? (Consider the type of activity, your motivation and the aspect of that memory that gave you the most satisfaction.)
- Think of a person you admire and list the positive attributes they have.
- List the finest qualities you have to contribute to the world. (For example: humour, compassion, wisdom, joy, sensitivity, creativity and so on.) Choose the two that are the most important to you.
- List your past activities and accomplishments that most accurately

reflect what you care most deeply about. Choose the two that are the most important to you.

- To define your purpose complete the sentence:
  I am a/an (two positive attributes) (two activities you enjoy).
  For example: I am a wise and joyful teacher and parent.
  This statement of purpose can provide a foundation for your specific goals.

CREATING A VISION

- Do you have a clear vision of how you would like your life to be? If not, create one: think about the various aspects of your life – relationships, family commitments, social life, personal, spiritual and professional growth, leisure time activities, time alone and making a contribution.
- Describe in writing how each aspect would look in an ideal scene (if you were living as you would like to be).
- How different is your 'ideal scene' from your current situation?
- What changes would you like to make?
- Set some specific goals in the various aspects of your life where you would like to create change. Write your goals as short, positive, present tense statements. Choose up to four or five goals to actively work on.

Having set your goals, review them by considering:
- Are your goals specific and measurable? How will you know when you have achieved them?
- Have you included a time limit?
- Are these goals manageable or do they need to be broken down into small steps?
- What little steps will you need to take? (Make an action plan in order of priority.)
- Are your goals in harmony with one another?
- Are they meaningful to you and aligned with your values and purpose?

- Visual images are powerful. To keep honing your vision and making it more believable make a dream poster, draw your dream or collect photos or cuttings resembling your accomplished dream and make a scrapbook.

COMMITTING TO ACTION

If you are embarking on a new venture, doing some research and reflecting on the possibilities is often an important first step.
- What information will you need to help you make an informed choice?
- Where will you gather the necessary information from? (Books, speaking with people, doing research etcetera.)
- What skills and knowledge do you need to gain in order to succeed?
- In what ways does your dream require you to grow?
- What obstacles to your venture can you foresee? How will you overcome these?

Having gathered the information, the following questions can help you make a definite decision about whether to proceed.
- Does your venture feel exciting and inspiring or overwhelming and frightening?
- How much energy do you have for it?
- Is it in keeping with your long term goals and overall life purpose?
- Is it worth investing your time, energy and money into?
- Does it feel right?
- What is your intuition telling you?
- Are you willing to pay the price this dream will require?
- How will your life be different when you've succeeded in this endeavour?

OVERCOMING DOUBTS AND FEARS

- Do you opt consistently for comfort at the expense of challenge, excitement and adventure because of self-doubt and fear?

- What role (if any) does your inner critic play in generating anxiety?
- If you experience a lot of anxiety is this coming from underlying issues from the past that need to be dealt with?
- When you contemplate your dream what are you most afraid of?
- How likely is it that these particular fears will eventuate?
- Will you allow your fears to stop you pursuing your goals or are you committed to finding creative ways to support yourself to overcome them?
- Do you need help with this? If so what form of help do you need and when will you put this in place?
- Make a list of your fears then go through your list one at a time and decide what specific strategies (if any) you need to put in place to help you feel more confident.
- Make a list of positive self-talk you can use to calm your fears. Refer to that list often.

MEETING THE CHALLENGE OF SETBACKS

- When you experience a setback do you usually tend to feel defeated or challenged?
- When difficulties arise are you inclined to stay focused on your goal or become over-focused on the obstacle?
- Do you tend to be optimistic or pessimistic; to focus on what you do have or what you don't have? How does this impact on your ability to overcome setbacks?
- How do you usually go about overcoming setbacks?
- What attributes do you draw on within yourself when you encounter setbacks?
- Have you experienced times when setbacks resulted in an even better outcome?
- Write about the times when you have encountered adversity and gone on to achieve success. Refer back to this as a reminder that all is well when you come up against a setback.

BALANCING COMMITMENT AND SELF-CARE

- Generally do you notice when you are getting tired, overwhelmed, stressed or upset and take active steps to care for yourself or do you tend to push on regardless?
- Do you have enough space in your life for the things that are important to you?
- When you plan your week do you allow time for rest/recreation?
- How long is it since you:
  - snuggled up with a good book?
  - had a massage?
  - relaxed and enjoyed doing nothing?
  - watched a funny movie?
  - took a holiday?
  - spent quality time with family and friends?
  - had some free time to do whatever you choose?
  - stepped outside at night and looked up at the stars?
  - engaged in a leisure time activity you truly love?
- Which (if any) of your needs are not being met: emotional, physical, intellectual or spiritual? How can you rectify this?
- What would make your life easier and more enjoyable?
- Make a list of self-care strategies you can use. Include things that can easily be incorporated into your daily routine and those which require more commitment. Keep adding to the list.
- Practise as many of the self-care strategies on your list as possible each day.

LISTENING TO INNER WISDOM

- How often do you sit quietly and reflect?
- Are you reasonably in touch with your feelings, needs and true desires or does too much external busyness distract you from knowing your inner world well?

- What benefits have you experienced when you have taken the time to reflect?
- What inspired ideas have you had in the past that you consider have come from your creative mind?
- Are you aware of your intuition? In what way do you experience it? Do you trust it?

SPEAKING OUT

- Are you satisfied with your communication skills or would you like to make some improvements? If so, how will you go about this?
- When you deliver an important message are you more likely to be remembered for the message you gave or the manner in which you gave it?
- Are you able to stand up for what you believe? Do you find this difficult?
- Do you feel comfortable saying 'no' to other people?
- How often do you interact with others from an assertive position of directness?
- When you deal with conflict are you most inclined to withdraw, become assertive and state your opinion or become aggressive?
- Generally do you most often use your power to encourage and uplift others or diminish and get your own way?

GATHERING SUPPORT

- List the people you consider to be part of your support team.
- Do you have enough like-minded, optimistic, caring, supportive people in your life? If not, what steps would you like to take to increase your support?
- What help do you need in achieving your goals?
- Make a list of people who may be able to help you who you have not previously approached. Challenge yourself to step out of your comfort zone to ask for what you need.

- If you don't already have one, would you benefit from spending time with a mentor, life coach or sharing resources with an ally?

HEALING THE PAST

- Do unresolved issues from the past prevent you from moving confidently forward? What are these issues?
- Do you find it difficult to get close to people because you lack trust?
- Do you at times criticise yourself harshly?
- Do you often experience intense feelings (hurt, sadness, rejection, anger and so on)?
- How often are you troubled by painful memories of your past?
- Generally do your relationships with others tend to be easy, distant, tense or difficult? What do you put this down to?
- Who really knows you? Have you told your life story to anyone?
- Do you sometimes find yourself triggered into behaving in ways you later regret?
- What steps do you need to take (if any) to resolve any unfinished business from your past?

ENJOYING THE REWARDS

- What rewards have you gained by pursuing your dreams?
- What have your dreams taught you about yourself?
- In what ways have you grown as a result of your endeavours?
- Does what you say match what you do?
- Generally are you inclined to act in accordance with your values and conscience?
- Are you treating people the way you would like to be treated?
- Are you satisfied you are living your life with integrity?

COUNTING AND SHARING BLESSINGS

- Make a list of the many blessing in your life and keep adding to it. Read it often.
- In what ways do you already share your blessings?
- In what other ways could you make a contribution on a small or large scale?
- As an elderly person how do you want to be living your life? How would you like others to see you?
- How would you like to be remembered when you are no longer alive?
- What kind of legacy would you like to leave?

BIBLIOGRAPHY

The following inspiring books are recommended by the women interviewed or the author:

Cameron, Julia, *The Artist's Way*, United Kingdom, Souvenir Press, 1994

Canfield, Jack, Hansen, Mark Victor and Hewitt, Les, *The Power of Focus*, Florida, Health Communications Inc., 2000

Carlson, Richard, *Don't Sweat the Small Stuff*, Australia, Bantam Books, 1997

Chopra, Deepak, *The Seven Spiritual Laws of Success*, Great Britain, Bantam Press, 1994

Collins, James, and Porras, Jerry, *Built to Last*, London, Random House, 1999

Covey, Stephen R., *The 7 Habits of Highly Effective People*, New York, Simon and Schuster, 1989

Covey, Stephen R., Merrill, A. & Roger, Merrill, Rebecca R., *First Things First*, New York, Simon and Schuster, 1994

Davies, Sonja, *Bread and Roses*, New Zealand, Random House, 1997

Davies, Sonja, *Marching On...*, New Zealand, Random House, 1997

De Bono, Edward, *The Mechanism of Mind*, London, Kape, 1969

Douglas, Kay & McGregor, Kim, *Power Games*, New Zealand, Penguin, 2000

Dowrick, Stephanie, *Forgiveness and Other Acts of Love*, Australia, Penguin Books, 1997

Estés, Clarissa Pinkola, *Women Who Run With the Wolves*, London, Rider, 1992

Hay, Louise L., *The Power is Within You,* Australia, Specialist Publications, 1991

Hay, Louise L., *You Can Heal Your Life,* Santa Monica, Hay House Inc., 1984

Hill, Napoleon, *Think and Grow Rich,* New York, Random House, 1960

Jeffers, Susan, *Feel The Fear And Do It Anyway,* London, Century Hutchinson, 1987

Jeffers, Susan, *End The Struggle and Dance with Life,* Australia, Hodder and Stoughton, 1996

Kehoe, John, *Mind Power into the 21st Century,* Vancouver, Zoetic Inc, 1997

Kehoe, John, *Money Success and You,* Vancouver, Zoetic Inc, 1998

Kiyosaki, Robert T., with Sharon L. Lechter, *Rich Dad Poor Dad,* Arizona, Tech Press, 1997

Lee, Blaine, *The Power Principle,* New York, Simon and Schuster, 1997

Matthews, Andrew, *Being Happy!,* Singapore, Media Masters, 1988

Matthews, Andrew, *Follow Your Heart,* Queensland, Seashell Publishers, 1997

McGinniss, Alan Loy, *The Power of Optimism,* San Francisco, Harper and Row, 1990

McGregor, Miriam, *Petticoat Pioneers,* Wellington, Reed, 1975

Orbach, Susie, *Towards Emotional Literacy,* United Kingdom, Virago, 1999

Robbins, Anthony, *Unlimited Power,* New York, Simon and Schuster, 1997

Schwartz, David J., *The Magic of Thinking Big,* New York, Simon and Schuster, 1987

Tracy, Brian, *Maximum Achievement,* New York, Simon and Schuster, 1993